Building Youth Ministry
in the Parish

Building Youth Ministry in the Parish

Jerome K. Finn

Saint Mary's Press
Christian Brothers Publications
Winona, Minnesota

This book is dedicated to all the young people who have touched my life and shown me the face of God over the years. It is dedicated especially to my own children—my new baby, Katharine Eileen, T. J., and Chrissy. My hope and prayer is that all our children grow in love to be happy, healthy, and holy.

This work would never have been completed without the encouragement and patience of several friends. I am grateful to these people:
- my best friend, my wife, Jill, who never gave up hope and who makes me feel so lucky
- Mike Carotta, my mentor, whose encouragement helped me see gifts I never knew were there
- and, finally, all the wonderful people at Saint Mary's Press, especially Fr. Bob Stamschror, who are so dedicated and diligent in order that the completed project is better than ever imagined and is truly a form of ministry

The publishing team for this book included Robert P. Stamschror, development editor; Karen J. Fisher, special editor; Mary Duerson Kraemer, copy editor; Gary J. Boisvert, production editor and typesetter; Proof Positive/Farrowlyne Associates, Inc., cover designer; Marcy Ramsey/Publisher's Graphics, illustrator; pre-press, printing, and binding by the graphics division of Saint Mary's Press.

The acknowledgments continue on page 117.

Printed in the United States of America

Printing: 8 7 6 5 4 3 2 1

Year: 1999 98 97 96 95 94 93

ISBN 0-88489-256-5

Contents

Introduction

How do you go about starting or reshaping youth ministry in a parish in the 1990s? Or maybe the question should be broader: What should we, as a Christian church, be doing for young people as we approach the millennium?

And what are the best structures and strategies for ministering to youth during these times? How do we best keep teenagers and young adults connected with the Catholic community in times of great change? How do we reach out to those who have not had any real connection with the church since their baptism? What do adolescents need and expect from the church in the midst of their busy and complicated lives? Such questions need answering. This manual is written to help answer them.

The Author

I write from my own experience of life, church, and culture, along with a youth ministry coordinator's understanding of the younger generation's experience of life, church, and culture. Additionally, some of the best youth ministry mentors around have shared their wisdom with me and have provided me with many insights.

I believe the time has come—that we have gained enough experience and done enough research and theorizing—to develop an effective, systematic approach to youth ministry.

The Book

While writing this manual, I tried to keep in mind parishes that range from the small rural parish, to the inner-city parish, to the large suburban parish. I tried to provide resources that can be adapted to many situations.

The organizational and planning models in this book are deliberately ideal. You may not need or be able to fulfill them in every detail. However, they can serve as reliable guides as you build your own structures and design your own planning processes. And they provide a good measuring stick for evaluating what you currently have in place.

The book has four main parts:

- Part A, chapters 1 and 2, takes a look at the world of the younger generation in the 1990s and at the way youth ministry is responding to the church's call to minister effectively to young people.

- Part B, chapters 3 and 4, focuses on the parish climate and organizational structures that root the ownership of the youth ministry effort in the parish community.
- Part C, chapters 5, 6, and 7, is on planning and maintaining an effective ministry to young people.
- The appendices provide some additional excellent foundational information that I have come across in my research.

Each chapter begins with a set of reflection questions. These questions can help you to read the chapter in light of your own particular circumstances and experience. Samples and handouts are located at the end of each chapter in which they are mentioned.

The Audience

Building Youth Ministry in the Parish is written for anyone who cares about young people and wants to ensure the best possible opportunities for them to be connected with the church and to benefit from the wisdom and support the church has to offer. This book is for all the following people:

- the *pastor or parish council members* who want to build a solid youth ministry in the parish
- the *full-time youth ministry coordinator* who wants to enlist wisely and effectively the gifts and talents of the people in the parish
- the *priest* who has chosen to or been assigned to work with young people, but is not sure where to begin
- the *leader of a particular youth activity or program* who needs a systematic approach to planning
- the *volunteer* who has limited time but wants to ensure that what time she or he does have for ministry among young people is used wisely
- the *parish member* who simply wants a better understanding of today's young people and the need for the church to respond to them

The Book's Underlying Principles

When I began writing this book, I sifted through files, readings, notes, and letters accumulated over more than twenty years of youth ministry. I recalled my personal conversion experiences as well. As I sorted through the evidence and memories of all that had taken place, I discerned ten principles that supply a rationale and direction for the organizational design and the planning processes given in this book:

1. Young people in today's society have many diverse personal and spiritual needs. Attending to both types of needs is critical to successful youth ministry.
2. Young people have incredible gifts and talents that can benefit the world and church today.
3. The Catholic church has a lot to offer young people, and it needs to offer those things to them.
4. Parishes and their leaders need to understand young people and make ministry to them an integral part of the parish mission.
5. The family is the primary influence on the formation of most young people. And supporting and strengthening the family supports and strengthens youth ministry.
6. Youth ministry, to be effective, needs to be comprehensive and well organized.
7. Young people have a variety of needs that are directly related to their spiritual, physical, and emotional development.
8. Youth ministry is most effective when it is done by a variety of people who share their gifts and talents with young people in a team approach.
9. Young people need caring adults in their lives who display the characteristics of servant and leader.
10. The spirit of God continues to touch young lives despite all our human weaknesses.

I believe that if these principles guide the building of youth ministry in the parish, then the Lord will be the real foundation and the main pillar of the ministry: "If Yahweh does not build the house, / in vain do the builders toil" (Ps. 127:1, *Psalms Anew*).

PART A

Foundations
for Parish Youth Ministry

CHAPTER 1

Challenges to Meet and the Church's Response

Questions for Reflection

- Think back on your own high school years. How is today's society different from when you grew up?
- In what way was your family important for you when you were growing up?
- Who were the most important persons for you and your family? What were their characteristics?
- What were some of the issues that caused stress or pressure for you as a teenager?
- What was your experience of church as a teenager? Did you feel that you were an important member of the parish community? Did you have a role model that helped you form your spirituality as an adolescent?
- What are some current myths you have heard about young people?

Changes and Challenges Facing Today's Young People

Maria was like most twelve-year-old, seventh-grade girls when she transferred to a local Catholic school at mid-semester—perhaps a bit quieter than others, but willing to get involved and ready to make new friends. Six weeks later she was found brutally murdered. The people of the small, quiet river town were shocked. Maria's classmates were terrified. What type of monster would do something like this to an innocent young girl? Surely drugs or some type of cult activity was a part of this. The community was even more shocked when those accused turned out to be two teenage girls. Their motive? Jealousy over a friendship.

Maria's story, which is true, is an extreme example of how the world of adolescents in the 1990s is an intensified—and more dangerous—version of the world most adults grew up in. For the most part, the needs of young people—security, a sense of belonging, autonomy, and the like—have not changed that much. But young people today often face them without the support of an attentive adult community and without values that could lead them to good and positive responses.

Our speeded up, media-intensive culture not only brings out these needs sooner, more frequently, and with more impact (often creating false needs) but also suggests horrible, self-destructive ways they might be dealt with—drugs and alcohol, early and promiscuous sexual activity, gangs, even murder. For young people, the future can be seen at one time as an exciting adventure and at another time as a terrifying maelstrom to be avoided or combatted.

Our adolescents are good kids with needs specific to the world they live in. The changes and challenges described briefly in this chapter help show why we need to take a new look at youth ministry—a look that can lead us to a ministry that adequately responds to the needs of today's young people.

Families

Growing up was fun on our farm near Starlight, Indiana. Our farm was part of the land that has been in our family since 1839. My grandparents lived just across the field, and on either side were aunts, uncles, and cousins. I experienced a tangible, visible connection with an extended family. Such a connection is not often available for children growing up today. In today's much more mobile society, many children grow up never knowing their grandparents other than from an occasional visit. Few young people can locate the graves of their ancestors. Self-identity and a sense of belonging and being rooted are eroded when young people cannot connect to their extended family, a locale, or their cultural heritage.

Children's sense of connection to family is further strained by divorce. Each year an estimated one million young people experience the divorce of their parents. Because of the high rates of divorce and remarriage, many of today's children live in stepfamilies. According to psychologist David Elkind, adolescents are most vulnerable to the identity problems often found in stepfamilies (*All Grown Up and No Place to Go*, p. 125).

Many children experience not only the emotional burdens of divorce but also the burden of increased household responsibilities. Most single parents have to work, and in situations where there are two parents, both often work outside the home. Returning from school to an empty house is common for many teenagers, who then might be expected to care for younger siblings or prepare supper.

Other social changes have had a profound effect on young people and their family life. Many families today are affected by a society that is addicted to satisfying human passions. When this is the case, unhealthy consequences result, such as losing the ability to be intimate without being sexual, misusing power, and abusing food or alcohol and other drugs. Physical and sexual abuse are increasing. A report given at a U.S. bishops' meeting in June 1992 states that one of every four girls will be sexually abused by the time she is eighteen, and one of every ten boys (*America*, 11 July 1992, p. 6).

Despite all the negative factors influencing the family, it is still the backbone of our society and the best support for young people. A study conducted by the Search Institute reports that in grades five through nine, the influence of parents is still stronger than peer influence (*Young Adolescents and Their Parents: Project Report* [Minneapolis: Search Institute, 1984], p. 50). More than ever, the church community needs to affirm and enable families as they raise their children.

Schooling

Until the last several decades, schools for the most part were small and personal. Students usually knew the other students and their families. But the trend in schools since the 1950s has been "the bigger the better." Schools have become so segregated according to age that children often only have a chance to relate to other children of the same age, children with the same problems and the same solutions. The variety of mentors who previously were available to students, such as older students and the teachers and administrators who worked with young people over a span of grades and ages, are no longer accessible on a day-to-day basis.

School used to be a place where young people were safe, where they could grow up, form an identity, and test their limits. But in many schools today, fights and other forms of violence are not uncommon. Some schools now have metal detectors at the entrances to locate weapons and armed guards patrolling the halls.

Peer Pressure and Vocational Pressure

The increased mobility of young people has extended the boundaries of peer groups way beyond the school and the local neighborhood. This is true even in rural areas where distance used to make it harder for young people to get together. Value systems far different from those they grew up with are within reach for most teenagers. Peer pressure has become mostly a negative force among teenagers, pushing them into harmful behavior, even gang activity.

Even pressure toward "positive" actions, such as choosing a career, adds stress at younger and younger ages. A surprising find in the Search Institute's study on the goals of young adolescents (those between the ages of ten and fifteen) was that to "get a good job" when they are older is a high priority. On average, getting a good job was the most important goal for boys and the second most important goal for girls (*Young Adolescents and Their Parents*, p. 139).

Myths About Young People

Young people's reactions to the greatly intensified environment of the nineties have given rise to a number of myths about them—myths that are often obstacles to youth ministry in a parish. These myths need to be dispelled, especially among adults who are in leadership roles. I have formulated some of these myths and offer for each one a dispelling example—one typical, I think, of many young people. The examples also offer hints as to the kind of ministry that breaks through the facades that give rise to the myths and reaches through to the real young person.

Myth 1: Young people don't care about anything anymore. Robbie, a sixteen-year-old, wrote the following note after attending a leadership training program:

> I was so grateful for the things we were taught. For so long I have had so much inside of me that I wanted to do. I look around and I see hunger, I see poor people, I see people without homes, and I want to do something about it. It just doesn't seem fair. A lot of times I look at my own life and the things that happen don't seem fair either. But I know that I am the only one that can change that. I really do want to make a difference. I want to be able to help people who need help. I now know that I have some skills to do that in some small way.

Young people do care. The task is to help them direct their energies in positive ways. In his book *Five Cries of Youth,* Merton Strommen identifies what he calls young people's cry of social concern. Teenagers and young adults genuinely care for people in need and want to help them. In the Search survey, 34 percent of Catholic young adolescents stated that they are concerned about world hunger and poverty (John Forliti, *Growing Together: An Opportunity for Young Adolescents and Their Parents*, p. 26).

Myth 2: You cannot communicate with young people. During the dance, fourteen-year-old Tammy sat next to the window and stared out of it. A couple of her friends were concerned that she was depressed because her family was going through a divorce. They said that Tammy never talks with anyone, even her peers. They felt sure she would not talk to an adult, but asked if I would try anyway.

Tammy's last name indicated that she might be related to a family I knew. I walked by and asked if she liked the band. She did. I sat down, introduced myself, and asked her name. Before long we found that one thing we had in common was growing up on a small farm. She soon was sharing a lot about her family, herself, and her life. A lot of what she said gave me a clearer understanding of what was going on in her life.

The problem is not that it is impossible to communicate with young people. The problem is that adults often come on with their own issues rather than listening for the teenagers'. Valuing young people and what they have to say is imperative.

Myth 3: Young people do not have faith. The following letter was written by a thirteen-year-old participant in a program of Christian initiation for teenagers. She wrote it while on a retreat during Holy Week before being baptized into the Catholic church:

> Dear God, I owe you everything because you have given me the most precious gifts of life and love. You are the reason for everything good, pure, and beautiful. I want to show you my thanks and praise by proving myself to you in every thought, word, and action of my daily life and by helping others to develop a stronger belief in you and telling them the mysterious ways you show me you are in my presence. I feel that this is now and will always be my biggest obligation in life: to try my very best to follow in your footsteps. . . . Lord, please bless me on my lifetime journey to do what is good and right. May I never become weak so that I can make you proud of your creation.
>
> Your devoted and loving friend,
> Amy

Teenagers have a faith that can move mountains. They need opportunities to express that faith, to question it, to have it affirmed, and to shape it as their own. They need adults who are willing to walk that faith journey with them, loving them along the way.

Myth 4: Young people do not have respect for adults. Lance was fourteen years old and certainly seemed not to respect anyone. He and his mother fought constantly, he had been thrown out of school, and he was in trouble with the police. One day while we were on a work project together, he shared some of his insights with me. In effect he was telling me the following:

> Nobody ever treats me like I am worth anything. My mom doesn't care, and to my stepdad I hardly exist. I hate my school counselor because he is unfair. He acts like I am not worth anything. In fact, if I would disappear from the face of the earth, I think he would be happy. You treat me like I am important, like maybe I've got something to say.

A wise man once gave me some advice about parenting. He said that I should treat each child as the particular individual that he or she is. From birth, each child is unique and has something unique to say. Do not discount the value of young people. They will give us the respect that we give to them.

Myth 5: Young people do not respond to discipline. Thomas is almost eleven. His mother, a single parent, recently shared with me the vast difference she has seen in his behavior within the last year. The reason she gave for this change was that they finally had been able to settle down and establish consistent schedules, mutually understood expectations, and clear limits.

Adolescents need structures that provide both sufficient room and clear limits. They are experimenting with new skills that test previous limits. They need enough allowance to explore while knowing the confines of safe boundaries. We can help them build discipline into their life if we provide reasonable and consistent freedom within reasonable and consistent limits.

Myth 6: The morals of young people are poor at best, and mostly nonexistent. Ronnie, a seventeen-year-old, wrote this:

We as Christians should love life in every way, shape, and form. We must take a stand on all inhumane acts against human life. Abortion, capital punishment, and war must not be a part of our lives, for life is God's most precious gift to us. We who possess this gift ourselves have no right to take it away from anyone else no matter what the circumstances.

Jesus broke through many of the barriers to love which often limit us in our relationships: selfishness, fear, prejudice, and resentment. Rather than possessing others, he proclaimed loving others as the greatest commandment. And he lived a life committed to being of service to others. We are told that Jesus loved and cared for everyone: the sick, the poor, the foreigner, and anyone who needed it. Jesus' idea of neighbor was anyone near. We must take this into account by breaking through those same barriers that Jesus did. We as Christians should overcome selfishness, fear, prejudice, and resentment and start loving and caring for everyone.

Keeping in view the positive behavior of the majority of young people is not easy. We are bombarded with negative statistics, presented in an alarming manner, about the morality of young people. When 20 percent of ninth-grade students are reported to have engaged in sexual intercourse, the 80 percent who chose not to are given little visibility or acclaim. Our society is geared toward catching someone doing something wrong and publicizing it. The best advice for working with young people that I ever received was in *The One Minute Manager:* "Help people reach their full potential. Catch them doing something right" (Kenneth Blanchard and Spencer Johnson [New York: William Morrow and Co., 1982], p. 39).

Myth 7: Young people do not care about tradition or heritage. Katie was an orphan in South Vietnam. She was adopted by a U.S. couple. Now, at age seventeen, she yearns to know more about her past. I recall her telling me the following:

Sometimes I dream that I am in a faraway land where everything is green and tropical. One minute I am a princess, and the next I am a little peasant girl in some village of grass huts. I wonder who my real mother and father were. I wonder if they were religious. I wonder what they believed in. It seems so distant, but yet it is so important to me.

Traditions and an awareness of one's heritage help provide a sense of stability, of being rooted, of belonging, and of identity. Teenagers, often secretly, appreciate and are proud of their heritage. We should not be surprised, though, if they do not demonstrate their heritage, because ethnic traditions and customs can run into conflict with peer acceptance. It is easier to be "just American." As adult youth workers, we need to enable young people to get in touch with their heritage. It is the essence of who they are as persons.

Myth 8: The peer group is the primary influence on young people. Krista, age seventeen, a talented and involved youth leader, spoke often of how she valued her family in the midst of growing up and coming into her own. On several occasions, she said that knowing that her mom and dad cared for her and cared about what she did was important to her. She wanted a relationship with them that, while recognizing her growing autonomy, did not diminish the value to her of their parenting.

As noted previously, it might not seem to be the case, but the influence of the family is still most important in the lives of young people. Youth ministry that gives attention to the family makes good sense.

The Church's Commitment to Youth Ministry

In the 1987 World Synod of Bishops, two propositions focused on the importance of young people and on the pastoral priority that this age-group should have:

Young people . . . are a very rich and unique reality. In their sensitivity they intimately perceive values such as justice, non-violence and peace. Their hearts are open to brotherhood, friendship and solidarity. They are greatly moved by causes that relate to the quality of life and the conservation of nature. . . . Young people have many things to say which all people can fruitfully listen to. (Proposition 51)

The church has much to say to young people. . . .

Pastors, therefore, should work out programs to improve the educational evangelization of young people. (Proposition 52, *Origins* 17 [31 December 1987]: 509)

In a similar fashion, Pope John Paul II addressed young people in 1985:

The first appeal I want to address to you, young men and women of today, is this: Do not be afraid! Do not be afraid of your own youth and of those deep desires you have for happiness, for truth, for beauty and for lasting love! Sometimes people say that society is afraid of these powerful desires of young people and that you yourselves are afraid of them. Do not be afraid! When I look at you, the young people, I feel great gratitude and hope. The future far into the next century lies in your hands. The future of peace lies in your hearts. (*Origins* 14 [10 January 1985]: 493)

The words of our primary pastoral leaders reinforce a long tradition of commitment to youth in the Catholic church in the United States—a tradition evidenced by Catholic schools, parish religious education programs, and the many Catholic youth organizations. Yet in the seventies, another call was added to the commitment, a call to consolidate the energies of separated programs into a holistic ministry to meet the needs of new generations of young people. The potential benefit of such a ministry to both young people and the church, and consequently to the whole of society, is immense.

The Call to Holistic Catholic Youth Ministry

The early seventies was a time of many crosscurrents in youth ministry in the United States. A lot of great minds were at work shaping a vision that would call for a holistic ministry to young people—a concept never before articulated in the Catholic church. Among the outcomes of these efforts were several documents from the youth ministry leaders that advocated holistic youth ministry. Two of these documents, *A Vision of Youth Ministry* and *The Challenge of Adolescent Catechesis,* will continue to have a great impact on youth ministry far into the future.

A Vision of Youth Ministry

In 1976 the United States Catholic Conference (USCC) approved the document *A Vision of Youth Ministry,* which pulled together a number of scattered and often separated ministries to young people and envisioned them being shaped into a holistic ministry. The shaping of holistic youth ministry that has been taking place since the writing of that document has gained enough reality and history to help us plan for a youth ministry that will serve well for the future. Rev. Thomas Gallagher, as secretary of the Department of Education, USCC, said in his preface to the tenth anniversary edition of the Vision paper: "Looking back over those ten years, it becomes quite evident not only that those purposes [reaffirming and recasting the church's ministry to young people] were achieved, but also that this truly visionary statement revitalized the Church's ministry with youth in this country."

The Vision paper set two primary goals that continue to guide youth ministry today:

1. "to foster the total personal and spiritual growth of each young person" (p. 7)
2. "to draw young people to responsible participation in the life, mission and work of the faith community" (p. 7)

The first goal focuses on the personal task of *becoming,* as adolescents mature in individual faith. The second goal deals with the interpersonal task of *belonging,* as adolescents participate in the community of faith.

In the article "Principles for Ministry with Youth" (*Network Papers,* no. 26 [September 1989]), John Roberto identifies a third goal that emerged after the Vision paper was initially written. He writes, "Youth ministry empowers young people to transform the world as disciples of Jesus Christ by living and working for justice and peace" (p. 2). This third goal focuses on the task of *participating* in the mission of the church to transform the world. These three goals, I believe, will continue to be primary goals for youth ministry as we move toward the year 2000.

The Vision paper lists a series of principles that underlie effective youth ministry and give it a character particularly its own. These principles need to be kept in view when planning youth ministry:

- "Youth is a unique time of personal development."
- "Youth ministry is concerned with the total person."
- "Youth ministry is rooted in relationships."
- "Youth ministry is a call to community."
- "Youth ministry proceeds as an affirmation of gifts."
- "True [youth] ministry duplicates itself."

(Pp. 8, 9, and 10)

Especially helpful for planning are the seven components of effective youth ministry that are identified in the Vision paper: word, worship, creating community, guidance and healing, justice and service, enablement, and advocacy (p. 12). I will talk about these components more specifically when I define the role of the youth ministry coordinator in chapter 6.

The picture of a holistic youth ministry is sharply focused and greatly enhanced by the document *A Vision of Youth Ministry.*

The Challenge of Adolescent Catechesis

Ten years after the first printing of *A Vision of Youth Ministry,* the National Federation for Catholic Youth Ministry, in collaboration with the USCC, the National Conference of Diocesan Directors of Religious Education, and the National Catholic Educational Association, published the document *The Challenge of Adolescent Catechesis: Maturing in Faith.* It calls for the incorporation of adequate formal catechesis into youth ministry as one of its essential components. In the document, adolescent catechesis is defined as a "systematic, planned, and intentional pastoral activity . . . directed toward the kind of teaching and learning which emphasizes growth in Christian faith through understanding, reflection, and transformation" (p. 5).

The document says, "the primary aim of adolescent catechesis is to sponsor youth toward maturity in Catholic Christian faith as a living reality" (p. 8). Two tasks for adults derive from this aim:

1. "to foster in youth a communal identity as Catholic Christians" (p. 8)
2. "to help them develop their own personal faith identity" (p. 8)

The first task, the Challenge document says, calls us to "present the faith convictions and values of the Catholic Christian tradition and invite adolescents to adopt and own these values and convictions." The second task involves us helping "adolescents respond to God in faith, in prayer, in values and in behavior" (p. 8). These two tasks relate closely with the youth ministry goals stated in the Vision paper.

The Challenge document also proposes ten principles for developing adolescent catechesis. The first five are foundational principles, in that they describe the key understandings that shape adolescent catechesis. The second five are operational principles that describe the process for developing adolescent catechesis. These ten principles are provided in appendix A, "Principles for Adolescent Catechesis."

Note that catechesis is to be an integral part of holistic youth ministry, not a separate function. Religious education, or catechesis, programs and youth group programs, typically separated in the past, need to be integrated into one whole ministry for the maximum benefit to the young people they serve.

Finally, the Challenge document presents faith themes most appropriate for the catechesis of both younger and older adolescents. These faith themes are provided in appendix B, "Faith Themes for Adolescent Catechesis."

Parish and Youth Together: Meeting the Challenge of Youth Ministry

The Resources of the Church for Youth Ministry

The Catholic church has a lot to offer young people, but we often sell it short. The church has a wonderful sense of tradition, ritual, and mystery that strikes a chord with the younger generation's experience of life and offers the opportunity for spiritual expression at this time in their lives. This quality of the church also reaches back and connects young people with the days when Jesus walked the earth. Young people often do not feel rooted in their own life, and the church can offer roots of faith that go deep and promise strength and vitality.

Also, the church is essentially a community—a people in relationship. One of the developmental needs of adolescents is having positive relationships both with peers and with adults. A church parish that is alive and vibrant can be a community of great support for young people, celebrating the important moments in their life through sacraments and providing reconciliation and comfort at times of pain. In formal youth ministry efforts, the church can offer all kinds of educational, recreational, and social opportunities that are grounded in Christian values and faith.

The Resources of Young People for the Church

Young people, in turn, have an incredible number of gifts they can bring to the church community. Their energy and vitality is life-giving. Their enthusiasm and idealism can get almost any task accomplished. Anyone working with young people realizes that they can have deep personal faith. My own faith has been freshened and deepened by the young people whose profound faith has touched my life. Their questioning has called me continually to question what it is I believe and why I believe it.

A survey of young Catholics in the United States and Canada reports that 82 percent of those surveyed feel close to God; 64 percent pray at least once a week, with half of those praying daily (Joan Fee et al., *Young Catholics: A Report to the Knights of Columbus* [Los Angeles: Sadlier, 1981], p. 8). Yet less than 20 percent of junior high students feel welcomed or accepted by adult members of their church (Eugene C. Roehlkepartain, "Why Jr. Highers Are Losing Faith," *Jr. High Ministry,* May–August 1990, p. 4).

This study of young Catholics is an example of a great deal of evidence indicating young people's openness to and desire for God's presence in their life as they face the many challenges to growing up whole. But at the same time, researchers point out that parishes need to take a new look at the way they are approaching young people and make a fresh start in youth ministry efforts.

CHAPTER 2

New Visions, New Blueprints

Questions for Reflection

- What kind of religious education did you receive when you were growing up?
- When you were a teenager, what kind of space was provided for young people in your parish? Did you belong to a church youth group? If so, how did you get in, and what did the group do?
- How did your family help you grow in faith?
- Describe the parish community that you grew up in. What stories do you remember about that community? What were your relationships with adults like? Who were the important people in your life? Were you able to talk with them about God?
- Have your attitudes toward racial and cultural diversity been affected by experiences you had when you were young?
- List some of the ways that you think the church can reach out to young people and help them stay connected with the church.
- If you were filling out a report card on your present parish, how would you rate the kind of environment it provides for the youth ministry program?

New Visions

Prior to the cultural changes discussed in chapter 1, the Catholic church's efforts in youth ministry presumed that young people would continue to live in a Catholic environment and would continue on in the Catholic faith of their parents. Youth ministry efforts focused on preparing young people to know what to believe and how to act as Catholic adults. The models were primarily programmatic and educational, such as Catholic schools and the Confraternity for Christian Doctrine (CCD), or recreational and social, such as the Catholic Youth Organization (CYO) and Young Catholic Students (YCS).

The church was mainly concerned with providing education that would retain a "purity of faith" and with creating environments where Catholic young people could meet and be with other Catholic young people. These efforts were built on a patriarchal and hierarchical model. Often the pastor delegated the responsibility for the youth program to the associate pastor. If lay adults were involved, it was primarily as teachers, leaders, and chaperones. They were seen primarily as helpers, not as sharers in ministry. In the mid-twentieth century, this approach to youth ministry generally met the needs of teenagers and the church.

But with the great cultural changes described in chapter 1 and the attendant rapid decrease of faith-commuting relationships, adults working with young people realized that a distinct shift needed to occur in youth ministry. This shift would respond to the ever-expanding world of young people and provide for the all-important faith relationships that were no longer adequately available in the usual and expected contexts, such as the family and the schools.

Relational Youth Ministry

A Vision of Youth Ministry and *The Challenge of Adolescent Catechesis,* discussed in chapter 1, recognized and gave impetus to the importance of relationships in youth ministry. Consequently, during the past fifteen years, ministry to young people has taken on a decidedly relational character. Youth activities and events have been offered in which adults, often parents themselves, could develop or strengthen personal relationships with young people. The adults involved were no longer seen only as teachers, leaders, or chaperones, but as committed, caring, faith-filled people who were there to help, support, enjoy, and value young people.

Vanishing quickly, too, was the idea of one person providing for the many and diverse needs of young people. A team approach became the preferred model in most instances—an approach that allowed young people to experience a variety of adult faith-lives rather than just one or two. Laypeople were realizing that the personal faith they possessed was a gift that needed to be shared now more than ever—with more young people than ever before. They found that in sharing their faith, they could help transform not only the lives of young people but also their own life.

This shift to a relational style of youth ministry, though perhaps motivated by the practical realities of passing on the faith, was grounded in the renewed theology of the Incarnation, the-Word-Made-Flesh, seen as God's decision to take up residence in us. This theology holds that we meet God in our relationships with others. Don Kimball, author of the book *Power and Presence,* applies this theology to ministry. His view is that the minister's first task is to do relational ministry—to be with, accept, and love people as God sees and loves them. He says the arena of relationships is where God happens to all of us and where the best ministry occurs.

Relational ministry, I am convinced, will continue to be a hallmark of youth ministry.

The Wedge Model

Working from a model first proposed by Lyman Coleman, Kimball developed a model of youth ministry that has become known as the "wedge model" (see figure 1). This model illustrates the connections between youth ministry and the faith growth of young people during their adolescent years. It has three distinct segments: (1) evangelization, the building of community; (2) catechesis, the handing on of the message of faith; and (3) vocation, the doing of service.

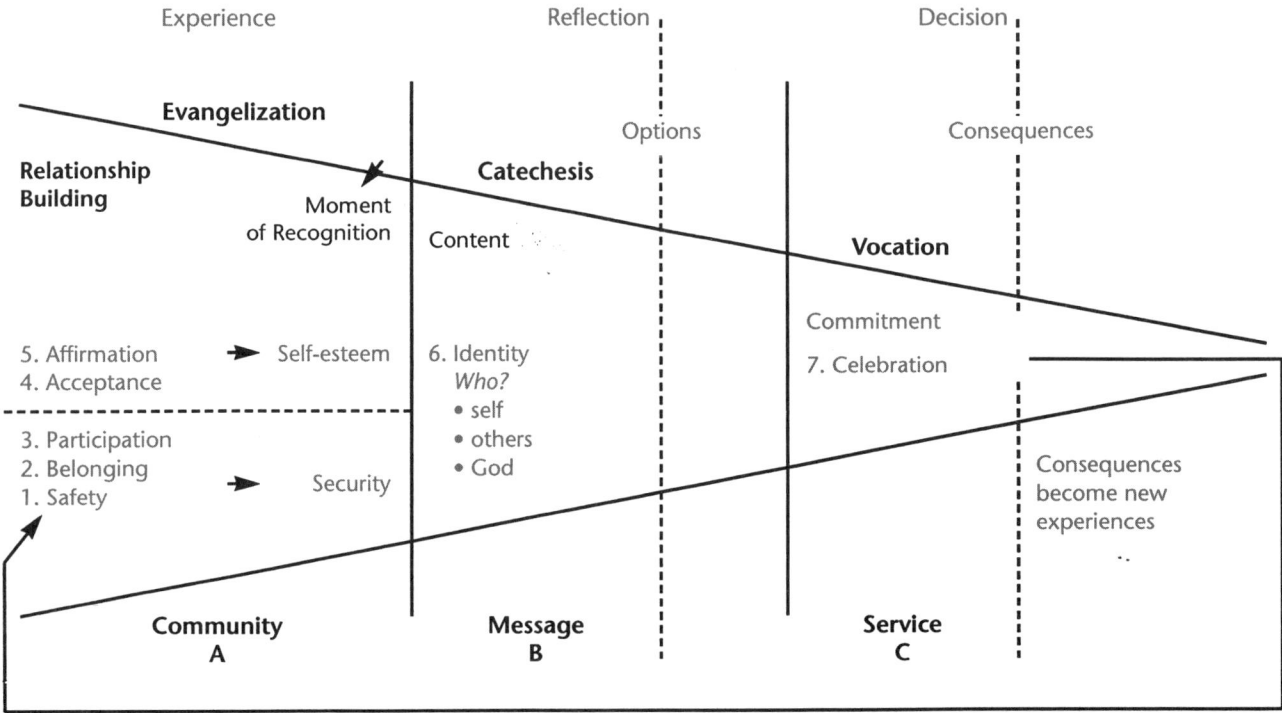

Figure 1. The Wedge Model

Reprinted by permission of Kimball, *Power and Presence,* p. 145.

Relational ministry is an essential dimension of all the segments of the model but is most prominent in the first stage—the stage of evangelization. Here it is seen as the ministry of affirming the young people and of building that trust and sense of belonging upon which all further youth ministry must be based.

Briefly, let's take a closer look at all three segments of the model and identify the elements that need to be present in them—elements that for the most part depend on establishing nurturing personal relationships.

Evangelization and community: To build community, five important elements need to be present: safety, belonging, participation, acceptance, and affirmation.

These five elements of community building can occur in a thousand different ways: in athletic events, lock-ins, retreats, social activities, celebrations, bereavement, and so on. If what you offer young people responds to their relational needs, they will get involved, and community will be built.

In the midst of the experience of community, something mystical occurs—a moment of recognition of God, or as Kimball puts it, the "aha moment." Through any number of ways, the young person realizes the presence of God in other persons, and especially in herself or himself. Once the presence of God is recognized, lives are transformed, and the individual moves into the next segment of the wedge.

Catechesis and message: The young person now wants to know more. What did Jesus say about God's loving presence? What does it mean to be a person who believes that God is present in oneself and in others? How does one live this faith and express it in church community? The primary element in this stage is catechesis. Catechesis can take the form of liturgical worship, the sharing of faith in scriptural study or prayer groups, formal instruction, and so forth—all forms whose effectiveness in handing on the message of faith depends on positive relationships between the ministers of catechesis and those being catechized.

Vocation and service: The final segment of the wedge model is that of commitment to service. The primary element in this stage is the desire to make a positive difference in the lives of people in need. Young people take what they have learned and share it with others. For many young people in a youth group, this is the time when they become peer leaders or peer ministers. Again, the desire to serve and the effectiveness of the service given is greatly determined by the quality of the relationships involved.

The Family

The family is the cornerstone of relational youth ministry. As the Vision paper states, youth ministry takes place in a variety of contexts. But no context is more important than that of family relationships. Young people can learn more about God from their relationship with their parents than from anything else in their life. While parents of today are becoming more confident of their positive impact on the faith-life of their children, they still count on formal youth ministry programs to help them in their role as parents and to provide that broader faith context needed as young people move from family relationships into a fast-changing world. At the same time, youth ministers realize that anything that can be done to strengthen family relationships is automatically a ministry to the young people who are in these relationships.

Some suggestions for this type of youth ministry are in appendix C, "Connecting Parents with Their Children." Also, the National Conference of Catholic Bishops (NCCB) has published a document stating that church leaders need to pay attention to developing a family perspective in policies, programs, ministries, and services. The directives in this document are pertinent to any planning for youth ministry and are provided in appendix D, "Developing a Family Perspective in Youth Ministry."

Multicultural Youth Ministry

The growing multicultural diversity in North America opens up many new opportunities for youth ministry. Marina Herrera, in an article entitled "Toward Multicultural Youth Ministry," describes what youth ministry will need to consider in the future: "I am firmly convinced that youth ministry must have a clear connection with cultural anthropology but not merely with reference to minority cultures but to the cultural patterns and understanding of the dominant groups as well" (John Roberto, comp., *Readings in Youth Ministry,* pp. 89–90).

Herrera proposes a number of principles that need to be present in a ministry to young people of minority cultures:

The principle of presence: Being present to minority youth means going out and meeting them in their environment. Only ministers who are not afraid to leave the boundaries of scheduled events and activities and go to the places where these youth work and play will be successful in inviting them to meaningful activities and supportive relationships. Peer ministry can be very effective here.

The principle of understanding: Being culturally literate means understanding the history, essential components, and most significant expressions of each ethnic culture, and relating well to the specific difficulties encountered by young people who are growing up in two different worlds of meaning and values. Cross-cultural relationships and communication skills are essential.

The principle of affirmation: Providing affirmation to young people of minority cultures means ministering in a culturally appropriate way and recognizing talents and personal assets that may not be valued by the mainstream culture (often the culture of the minister). Cultural literacy that includes being familiar with cross-cultural styles of learning, motivation, and reward is essential.

The principle of challenge: Only by recognizing and overcoming the prejudices and limitations imposed by the minister's own cultural perspectives can one recognize and challenge the prejudices and limitations of the other cultures. Herrara says, "Educators and ministers of minority youth must be objective in the evaluation of cultural accomplishments of all the groups that are present in society and recognize the shortcomings of the dominant culture. Only then will they be able to call forth minority youth to overcome the shortcomings of their own cultures and bring them to the full potential of their humanity" (Roberto, *Readings in Youth Ministry,* p. 97).

The value of multicultural awareness in youth ministry will be recognized "when youth groups are able to join hands across cultural or racial barriers and give witness to their hope for a more just and peaceful world," Herrera says (Roberto, *Readings in Youth Ministry,* p. 101).

The Expanded Age Range of Youth Ministry

Along with the growing recognition in the seventies and eighties of the importance of relational and multicultural youth ministry, youth ministers also began to recognize that the formational consequences of cultural change on faith development are taking place earlier in young people's lives and lasting longer. It became clear that the holistic ministry needed to meet the faith goals laid out in the Vision paper and the Challenge document could no longer be limited to young people in high school. A holistic youth ministry also needed to reach out to early adolescents (ten- to fifteen-year-olds) and to young adults (eighteen- to thirty-year-olds). Early adolescent youth ministry and young adult ministry have now become established dimensions of youth ministry.

Youth ministry today not only targets young people in this whole age range but also regards all the facets of their life and walks with them in their faith journey—physically, spiritually, emotionally, and intellectually. People in this broad range of ages have specific and diverse developmental needs that coincide with all these areas of human life. Recent research has provided useful descriptions of these developmental needs. A version of the descriptions is offered in appendix E, "Developmental Needs of Adolescents and Young Adults."

Keeping in view the entire age range and the whole scope of developmental needs is important for all aspects of planning youth ministry, especially when planning particular events and activities.

New Blueprints

The picture of youth in today's world and the ministry to them as projected by church documents clearly calls for new blueprints and new designs. Youth ministry can no longer be carried out through an approach in which the pieces operate as independent and unrelated functions. Rather, the approach now needs to be both comprehensive and integrated.

A Program Model for Total Youth Ministry

My own introduction to total youth ministry programming took place during a course on leadership in the Certificate of Youth Ministry Studies Program offered by the Center of Youth Ministry Development.

Brian Reynolds, an instructor, first talked about two older styles of ministry to young people. He described one style in which the focus was on the youth group. A dynamic youth group program might include an occasional opportunity for catechesis, a retreat, and maybe even a service project. Yet the focus was on maintaining the group, with group membership as the central goal. For example, as a teenager, my youth group had specific rules, expectations, membership dues, and even a membership card. If you were not a regular member of the group, you were not welcome at the youth group's activities.

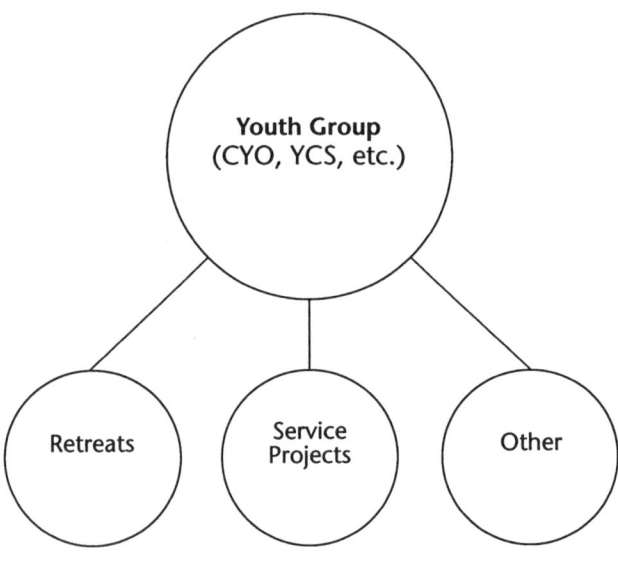

Figure 2. Youth Group

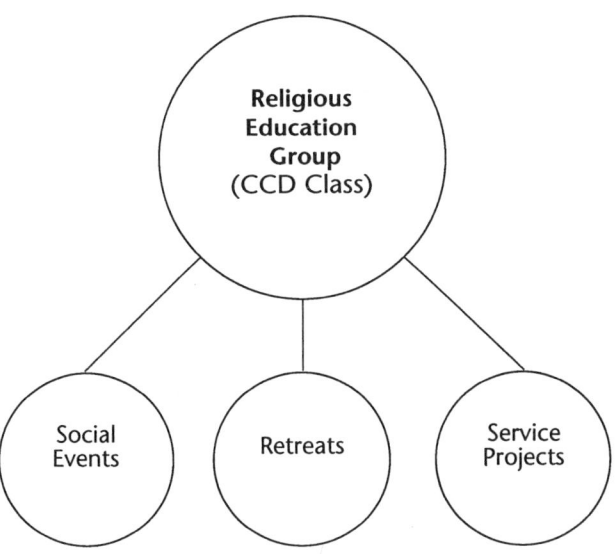

Figure 3. Religious Education Group

A second style focused primarily on religious education. True, those attending religious education classes occasionally might socialize together, go on a retreat, or perform a service project. But the primary reason for meeting was religious education, with other activities being supplementary to and supportive of religious education goals.

Reynolds then described a model that looks like the spokes of a wheel and includes a myriad of opportunities for young people. Social activities, retreats, confirmation classes, athletics, leadership development, and parental involvement are all part of this picture, a picture of total youth ministry. The youth group and religious education group are included as spokes of the wheel, as parts of a total youth ministry rather than being total youth ministry in and of themselves (see figure 4). The parts of the total youth ministry program cover three main aspects: proclaiming the Christian message, building community, and inviting commitment.

Reynolds went on to describe how the different parts of a total youth ministry program respond to the variety of youth needs. Some young people need a close-knit group. Others may not want to be a group

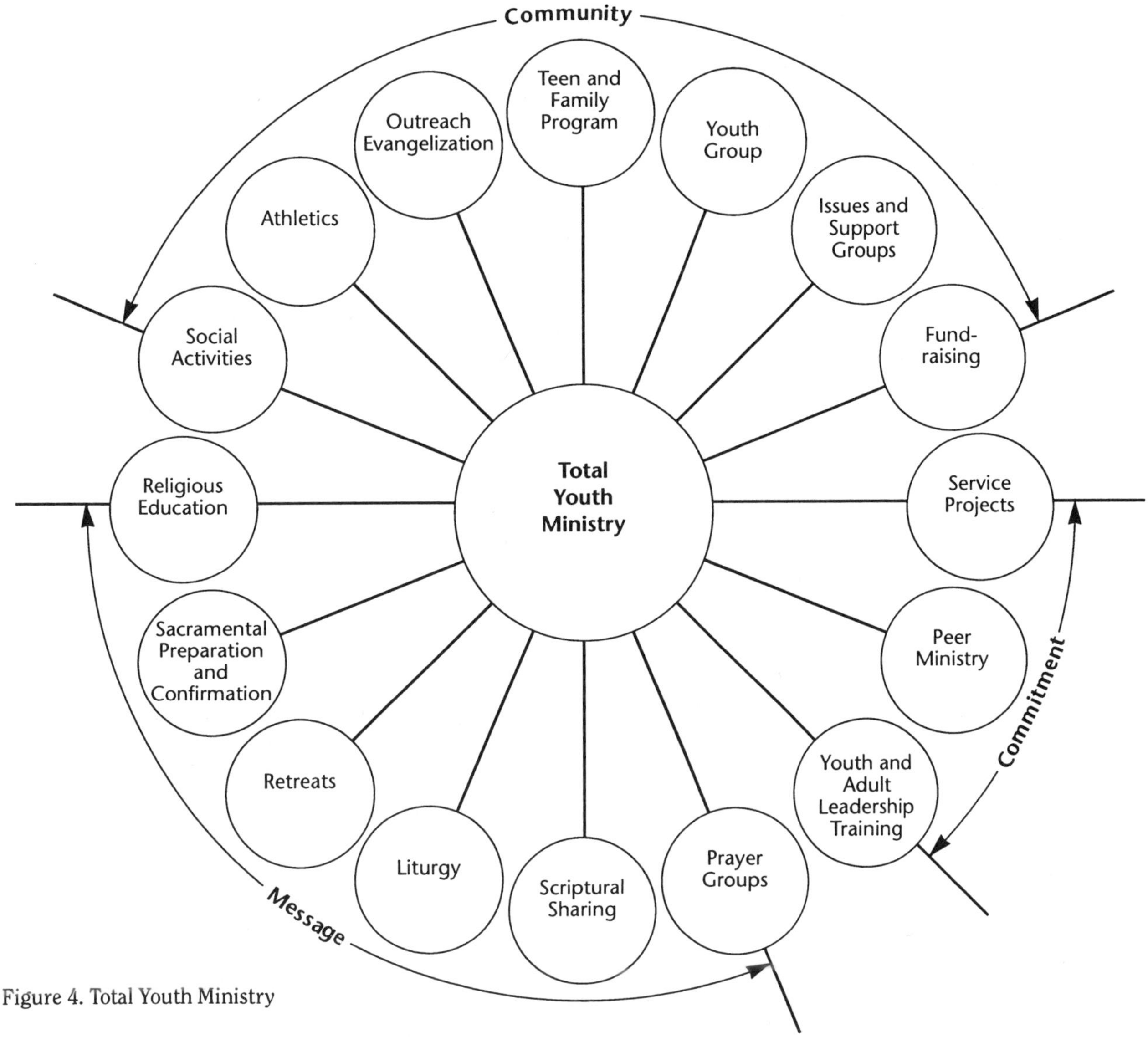

Figure 4. Total Youth Ministry

member but may want and need a retreat. Still others may desire a service opportunity or a good religious education class. Actually, most young people at some time during their life may want to participate in most of the opportunities of a total youth ministry, but not all at the same time.

For years I could never understand why I had 150 young people attending religious education, but when I had a CYO meeting, I was lucky to get 50. I kept wondering what I was doing wrong. Why would young people get involved in religious education and not in the youth group? Why did some young people who went on retreats never show up at youth group meetings? Why did some young people who helped out with service projects never come to a social activity?

It was like a light coming on when I realized that any one particular program or event might not be a need of theirs, at least not at that time. I did not need all the young people coming to all the activities all the time. These teenagers and young adults had a diversity of needs and wanted a parish program that they could plug into based on their needs.

By the time Reynolds finished the program, I had a whole new picture of what parish total youth ministry should look like. When I started adding up the number of young people who were involved in the many different activities in my parish, the numbers grew significantly. After that, when people asked (as they are apt to do), "How many young people are involved?" I could honestly say, "All of them." Even if it was only by way of receiving the newsletter, the young people were aware that the parish offered opportunities for them any time they needed them. I welcomed their participation in anything connected with the church. Yet I knew I had to respect their freedom to choose. I had to respect where they were at on their own faith journey, all the while inviting a deeper involvement in the life of the faith community.

In providing this kind of total youth ministry, the church makes a visible commitment to be available to young people. The wisdom and benefit of this kind of commitment was confirmed for me one day when I met two college students from out of town. They were from a parish where a good friend of mine was the youth ministry coordinator. When they found out that I knew Mary, they went on and on about what a wonderful job she did for the parish. They talked about how present she was to young people and how diverse her programs were. They had nothing but praise for her.

Some time later, when talking with Mary, I told her what the students had said. When she heard who the students were, she burst into laughter. She said that these two students had never once come to a parish youth ministry activity in their four years of high school. Yet they were positively affected by it and were sincere about the affirmation they had for the parish and the youth ministry program.

It struck me that because that parish provided a variety of opportunities, these students felt welcome to attend at any time—even though they chose not to attend. They appreciated what was being done, even if they did not get involved. Invitation, a form of evangelization, by way of availability can have more positive outcomes than is often realized.

This approach does not mean that we should not challenge young people to see beyond their own needs. The three primary aspects of youth ministry are equally important: community, message, and commitment.

Young people are more receptive when ministry is based on their needs. Pastoral ministry uses their needs as a foundation, but also includes our own wisdom and experience to round out a more holistic dimension to youth ministry. Providing only what they want based on their perceived needs would be like only serving pizza, hamburgers, and fries for them to eat. Their diet needs to be balanced, including various types of vegetables, dairy products, and so on. We need to be creative in getting them to be open to "trying new foods" that will be healthy for them. Catechesis, community, or service may need to be added to their "diet" so that their growth and maturity in faith is healthy.

Jesus provided us with a good example of how to minister in a holistic and engaging way. He built relationships, welcomed involvement, and challenged others to participation and commitment out of love and compassion.

Parish Ingredients for Total Youth Ministry

Within the parish a mix of ingredients is needed as a firm base to support the total youth ministry wheel and to keep it from getting mired down. When I was trying to identify these ingredients, I asked the opinion of the young people in my parish. Much of what follows comes from them.

Caring Adults

The young people left no doubt that the single most important ingredient for effective youth ministry is adults who choose to get personally involved with them—adults who believe that young people are important enough to commit time and energy to, and adults who understand and respect them.

Adults who work with young people are sometimes surprised at the great impact a relationship with a young person can have on both the young person and themselves. Any genuine relationship involves a dynamic exchange. But in a relationship between an adult and a young person, the energy flow from the young person to the adult is especially high. Young people respond with their whole being—physically, emotionally, sexually, and spiritually.

Recently, I assembled a committee to organize an anniversary celebration. A young woman I had not talked to since she graduated from high school, about ten years previously, responded to my bulletin invitation. At the opening meeting I asked the people each to introduce themselves and share a little bit about how their involvement in youth ministry had made a difference in their life. When Paula spoke, she mentioned a lot of wonderful memories that she had of her teen years. She went on to say that two people had affected her more than anyone else: her husband, and me.

I could not believe what I was hearing. Here was someone I had not seen in ten years who was naming me as one of the two primary influences in her life. I felt a mixture of surprise, embarrassment, and pride. I had no idea that I had so significantly touched her life.

Paula's sharing of this information startled me into two realizations. The first was how profoundly we, as adults, can touch a young person's life, often without being aware of it. To realize that influence can be humbling as well as frightening. Second was how much young people are looking for adults who genuinely care for them—adults who accept them as persons, even though they may not agree with all their actions.

Parish Community

When I say that community is an important ingredient for effective youth ministry, I am referring to community in the parish at large. I am distinguishing it from community among the young people themselves, that is, the experience of belonging to a group of peers among whom they feel safe, welcome, and accepted.

Can effective youth ministry succeed without a sense of community in the larger parish? For example, confirmation of adolescents is seen as a celebration of a young person's initiation into the parish. But do our teenagers see the parish as a place where they really want to belong? Does the parish seem open, loving, and life-giving? Is it a place that is safe for them—a place where they can safely express their faith? Are parish liturgies attractive and relevant to young people, and do they challenge them to grow spiritually?

I have heard many stories in which a vibrant youth ministry, lacking the support of the larger parish community, ended in disaster for the young people involved in it. Once the young people had outgrown the youth community, they found little opportunity in the larger parish to exercise the leadership skills they had gained, no place to adequately express the faith they had nurtured, no sense of being needed as people integral to parish life. These young adults often went to places and groups where they did feel needed, leaving the parish or even the Catholic church.

On the other hand, even if the parish is not an ideal community, it does not mean that nothing can be accomplished in youth ministry. With proper leadership the young people in a youth group can become future transformers of a parish into a life-giving community. Rather than allowing them to become decriers of a lack of parish community or to become disillusioned, they can be challenged to take on leadership roles in helping to bring about positive changes.

Communication

The lifeline of community is communication, not only communication within youth community boundaries but also communication between the youth community and the larger parish community. Publicity and public relations are an important part of youth ministry, yet this is an area that often falls short.

Effective communication between the youth community and the larger parish community can happen. Newsletters, mailings, phone contacts, and parish bulletins can serve well. Activities in which the youth community and the larger parish community can be involved together, such as liturgies, service projects, and parish parties, are especially effective. The broader the base of communication, the better. Not only should young people be aware of what is going on in the parish as a whole, but everyone in the parish should be aware of what is going on in the youth ministry and in the lives of the young people.

Good and effective communication can also help the parish gain a sense of ownership of its ministry to youth, help parishioners understand youth issues, and help parishioners realize the extent to which the church at large is committed to connecting young people to its life and its mission. Communication and community building go hand in hand.

Budget-Backed Regard for Youth Ministry

Another ingredient needed for nurturing a viable youth ministry is a high regard by the parish for the ministry and those in it. This regard, to be authentic, needs to grounded in a willingness to support the youth ministry with the money necessary to do a good job. The youth ministry commission, whose establishment and function is described in chapter 4, can have an important role in stirring up this support. Along with ensuring an adequate budget, it is also important for the commission to give the young people opportunities both to help plan the budget and to raise some of the money for it. Budgets are discussed further in chapter 4.

Space

A good environment for young people gives them space to be and space to grow. A viable youth ministry needs a space that young people can call their own—a space to gather, to meet, to have quiet conversation, to listen to music, or to just hang out and do homework. It should be clean, bright, and attractive. The ideal space would be a youth center furnished with a stereo, a television and VCR, a table with chairs, a typewriter or two, computers that students could use, a game area, refreshments, and so forth.

Space for youth ministry should also include an office where youth leaders can work. The office should be equipped with a desk, file drawers, and a phone. Such an office is especially necessary in parishes that employ a paid coordinator for youth ministry.

Total youth ministry programming reinforced with a parish environment that supports youth ministry speaks a loud, clear message to young people that says: "We care about you. We want you to feel welcome here. We want you to know that you are very important to us." In effect you tell your young people that without their presence, you are less than whole. Without their vital link in the chain of generations that make up your church, you are a broken community.

Admittedly, new visions and new blueprints for youth ministry can appear to be overwhelming. But having them is an essential first step. And remember, putting them into action does not need to be done all at one time, nor can they be carried out by only one or a few people. In the next chapter, along with looking at the framework for youth ministry, we will look at the work force that is needed.

PART B

The Setup
for Parish Youth Ministry

The Framework and the Work Force

Questions for Reflection

- Does your parish have a pastoral council? How is it structured?
- Does your parish provide opportunities for input by persons interested in the workings of the youth ministry efforts?
- Who are the people in your parish that work in youth ministry? What are their titles and roles?
- To what extent do volunteers make up the work force of youth ministry in your parish?

The Parish Framework

Detecting a Missing Link in the Parish Framework

It never ceases to amaze me how God works through us and accomplishes so much despite our own agendas. The way that I stumbled upon an organizational link that was missing in many parish structures, a link that is key to transforming youth ministry, is one such example of God at work in our world.

I had been involved in youth ministry in the New Albany Deanery of the Archdiocese of Indianapolis for several years when I decided it would be a good idea to visit the twenty deanery parishes and see what their youth programs looked like. My first move was to send a letter to each parish asking for an invitation to some youth event—a youth group gathering, a leadership meeting, a planning session, or whatever. A year went by with no invitations.

The following year I sent another letter asking each parish to invite me to one of their meetings. Still no invitations! I began to get worried. And had my ego not been intact, I probably would have been concerned about whether I had any respect! As I thought about the situation, I realized that I was viewed by parish youth ministers as "the expert." So having me sit in on their activities would be like having the principal sit in on a class they were teaching. I decided not to issue a third request to be invited.

The third year I took a different approach. This time I sent a letter to the parish youth coordinators or other contact persons in the parishes and told them what day I was coming. I told them that I wanted to gather with anyone in the parish who in any way was connected with youth ministry: pastoral council members, board of education leaders, youth group leaders, adults working with young people, liturgy committee members, Saint Vincent de Paul Society members, the administrator of religious education, the school principal if they had one, the leaders of fellowship groups, and young people and parents—those involved in youth ministry programs and those who were not. I also told them that the purpose of the gathering would be to look at what they felt the needs were for the young people in their parish. If the date that I had given them was not convenient, then we rescheduled.

When each group gathered, we worked through several agenda items: a holistic needs-assessment survey, a brainstorming session, and a summary evaluation. (This meeting agenda and the survey can be found in sample 3–A, "A Process for a Parish Visioning Experience," and handout 3–A, "Parish Youth Ministry—Where Does It Stand?")

A youth ministry needs-assessment: During the first part of each meeting, everyone filled out a needs-assessment of the parish's youth ministry. I had developed it in light of the components of youth ministry as given in *A Vision of Youth Ministry*.

The assessment takes a holistic approach, an approach that many of those attending my gatherings were not familiar with. Many of the parishes are small and rural, and their youth ministries are composed mainly of youth groups. I used the assessment to help them see the work they did with young people in light of the holistic and comprehensive picture that the Vision paper presents. When everyone finished the assessment, I collected the results and took a few moments to react to them, again trying to project a picture of holistic and total youth ministry.

A brainstorming session: The second part of each evening was directed to dreaming and visioning. I asked the people what they would like to see going on for the young people in their parish in three years. I asked them to dream and envision without worrying about budgets, personnel, or resistance. My question was, "If there were no limits, what would you like to see happening for the young people of the parish three years from now?" I had them write each dream on a separate sheet of paper.

When the participants finished dreaming and writing, they taped their papers on the wall beneath one of four headings: Programs, Personnel, Resources, and Other. After all the responses were posted, we spent some time reading them privately.

What showed up on the walls was remarkable. The concern for young people was obvious, and the participants offered good ideas on what they would like to see happening for them. Surprisingly, many of the ideas were similar, whether they came from the seventy-six-year-old from the altar society or the sixteen-year-old involved in the youth group.

After everyone had an opportunity to see the dreams, I asked, "What types of resources does the parish and local community already have that would help you make your dreams come true in three years' time?" The group then brainstormed, and I wrote on newsprint the skills, talents, facilities, and other resources they identified.

My next question was, "What problems or roadblocks would your parish have to overcome to achieve your dreams?" Again they brainstormed as I wrote.

A summary evaluation: At the close of each meeting, I did a summary evaluation of what we had done and made recommendations based on what I had heard from the group. Those who were involved thought that the meetings were great and that a lot was accomplished. But time and time again I heard the questions, "Where do we go from here? How can we make sure that three years from now we won't be rehashing the things we have dealt with tonight?"

The Missing Link: Something More Than Planning Alone

Before explaining any further, I need to admit that I had a hidden agenda when I went into the parishes, and the recurring question, "Where do we go from here?" opened the way for what I wanted to happen. You see, I was convinced that a major problem in youth ministry was ineffective planning. I wanted these parish meetings to be the initial step to get a planning process started. But as I listened to people, *I realized that something besides planning was missing.*

I found that many parish programs depended on the initiative of one or two people. When these people got tired or burned out or moved on, there was nothing to keep the youth ministry going, and often it was a matter of starting all over again. Also, the parishes had little ownership of their ministry to young people. Ownership had been handed over to someone who was willing to do youth ministry. This person often had little or no connection with or accountability to the parish structures.

This is not to say that these parishes were completely ineffective in their ministry to young people. On the contrary, most parishes had some good youth ministry events and activities in place. But they tended to be independent of one another and to lack continuity. And with each new youth minister the events and activities changed. The need was not to *introduce* youth ministry to the parish; the need was to make youth ministry as integrated and consistent as possible.

To do this, something even prior to planning was needed—something that would not only provide comprehensive and integrated planning but also ensure the implementation and continuity of the youth programming that was planned. *The missing link that would ensure the continuity and comprehensiveness of youth ministry needed to be a piece in the parish structure that would provide an ongoing connection between youth ministry and the overall pastoral ministry of the parish.*

I had to go back to the drawing board and figure out how parishes could develop a structural piece that could not only plan but also root a comprehensive youth ministry in the mission and ministry of the parish.

Conceptualizing the Missing Link for the Parish Framework

From my meetings in the parishes, I realized that most of them already had organizational structures that were influenced by the Second Vatican Council's call for lay responsibility and collaboration in directing parish life. Most had a pastoral council with its various commissions, a finance council, and usually a board of education. However, youth ministry was seldom visually present in organizational charts, and if it was, it was loosely connected (see figure 5).

In this diagram of a typical parish, the youth ministry effort seems to be floating off to the side, with little official representation in the parish governing structure. When this is the case, youth ministry financing, leadership, planning, and so forth, takes place outside of the parish's overall pastoral effort. Consequently, youth ministry receives little real support from the parish and has little accountability in return. The only time the parish as a corporate body is inclined to give youth ministry any priority is when there is a perceived problem. My task was to envision some type of group that could sponsor youth ministry and at the same time officially link youth ministry to the governing parts of the parish's organizational structure.

Looking at what some parishes already had done to accomplish this task and conceptualizing what might work best, I came up with the concept of the *youth ministry commission* as the missing link. I recommended to each parish that they develop such a commission.

In the next chapter, I will describe in detail the youth ministry commission—the missing link—and situate it within a parish's overall framework. But before I do that, I want to describe the work force and organization needed for total youth ministry.

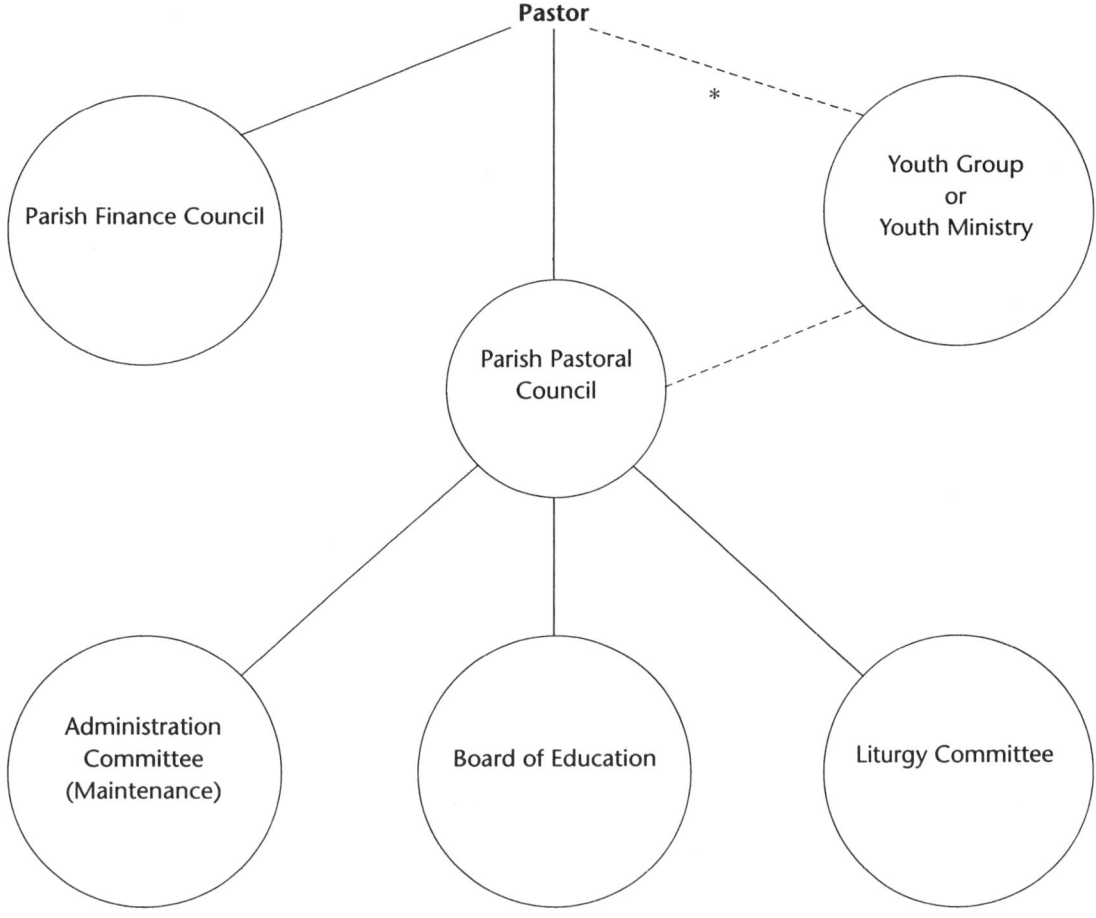

Figure 5. The Structure of a Typical Parish

*Dotted lines are used because often there is little connection between youth ministry and parish life.

The Work Force

To help form a picture of the work force for and organization of total youth ministry in a parish, look at figure 6. This diagram shows the work force is within the circle of the parish, whose members have a commitment to ministry for their youth. An obvious interconnection exists between the different roles in the work force, with the youth ministry coordinator being the hub that connects them all.

The Youth Ministry Commission

The youth ministry commission is a group of young people and adults who are representative of the parish. Its purpose is to ensure that total youth ministry is an integral part of the pastoral ministry and mission of the parish. (As mentioned, chapter 4 more fully describes this commission.)

The Coordinator of Youth Ministry

Every organization needs a designated leader. The coordinator of youth ministry in the parish is just that.

The title "coordinator" indicates that in a total youth ministry approach, the youth ministry leader coordinates, rather than tries to do or direct, all the activities and events of a total program. The coordinator might well staff or lead *some* of the youth ministry events and activities, but the primary task of the coordinator is to coordinate activities and events that other people are staffing or leading. The coordinator also trains, supports, and evaluates the people doing the work of youth ministry in his or her parish.

Depending on a parish's size and resources, it might hire a coordinator or seek a volunteer, either of which could be a full- or part-time worker. Or several parishes may combine to hire a coordinator together. The position of a coordinator is discussed in detail in chapter 6.

Leadership Teams

A total youth ministry approach also calls for teams of leaders to oversee events and activities. If the youth ministry efforts are organized according to the wedge model categories of community, message, and service (see chapter 2), it would be ideal to have three leadership teams, each one heading up the events and activities for a different category. For example, the *community team*

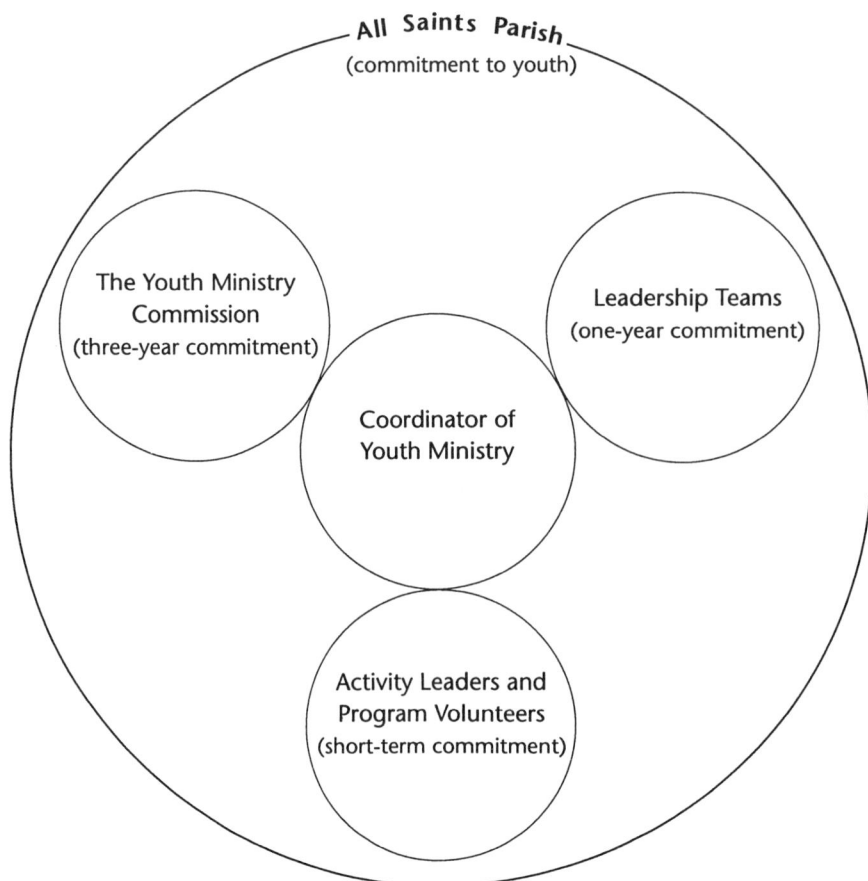

Figure 6. The Organizational Aspects of Total Youth Ministry

would be responsible for athletics, social activities, outreach, and the like. The *message team* would be responsible for faith-formation events such as catechesis, retreats, and liturgies. The *service team* would be responsible for peer leadership training, parental involvement, service and justice efforts, and so on.

Members of a leadership team are expected to make at least a yearlong commitment to the youth ministry effort. Their task is to make sure the activities and events scheduled in the area of their responsibility are well planned, staffed, carried out, and evaluated.

I have worked with a lot of different team models, and the one that I have found most effective has an adult and a youth member working together in a mentor and apprentice relationship. When an adult and a young person work together, some wonderful dynamics can take place. Adults have to make sure they do not try to do everything. Young people need opportunities to learn skills, and adults can help them learn. Oftentimes young people (and adults) have trouble making commitments and following through with responsible action. Good adult team members can gently call youth members to accountability. Being on a team gives adults an opportunity to share their faith and lets the young people see the adults as people who genuinely care. In return the young people rejuvenate the adults with their enthusiasm and energy.

The experience of Kyle is an example of a positive outcome of an adult-youth team. Kyle was fifteen years old when he became a member of a youth ministry leadership team. On a Christmas card he sent to an adult leader he had worked with, he summarized some of his feelings about that experience:

> We've known each other for just under a year now. What's ironic about it is that in this short amount of time, we've become the best of friends. To me you're the big brother that I never had. You've taught me so much. I feel as though I could tell you anything and you would understand. I thank God for the blessing of our friendship. Thanks for being there for me. I love you.

Activity Leaders and Program Volunteers

Activity leaders and program volunteers are the doers of the youth ministry program. Activity leaders head up specific activities. They are the coaches, the catechists, the dance directors, the camping trip leaders, the soup kitchen organizers. Volunteer helpers staff particular events and activities, bake the pizzas, decorate for the party, bring the cookies, clean up, and so on.

These folks are the hands and feet of youth ministry and make a clear, unmistakable statement to the young people that the parish cares for them.

The commitment of activity leaders and program volunteers is short-term. For example, an activity leader might head up a confirmation reception; when that event is finished, so is the leader. Likewise, a program volunteer might bake pizzas just for that confirmation reception. We need to make it clear to these leaders and volunteers that they are committing their time and energy for a short term, for a single event. They need to know that they will not have to be baking pizza for the next ten years every time pizza is on the menu for a youth event. Being an activity leader or a program volunteer is a good opportunity for some direct one-on-one ministry.

If you have been adding as you read, you may be thinking that dozens of people are needed to run a total youth ministry program. And I readily admit, dozens may be needed at a large parish. Before you give up on this approach to a work force for youth ministry because of the number of people needed, read chapter 7, which goes into greater detail about recruiting these volunteers and providing the support they need in their ministries. Getting enough volunteers to carry out a total youth ministry effort may not be as difficult as it first seems.

With a picture in mind of the parish framework within which youth ministry takes place and of the work force needed for youth ministry, chapter 4 takes a more thorough look at the youth ministry commission that links the two together.

The following is a sample process for a parish visioning experience. Such a meeting is intended to surface youth ministry needs and hopes while also communicating a comprehensive picture of total youth ministry to the participants.

The process is designed for gatherings of people who represent the variety of parish organizations, agencies, and individuals that are involved with or have concerns about the parish's youth ministry.

Introduction
Welcome the participants. Have them introduce themselves to the group by giving their name and their involvement with youth ministry. Give a brief history of why the meeting was called and a preview of what will take place.

Opening Prayer
Call the people to prayer and provide the opportunity for people to pray for success in the tasks to be completed at the meeting.

Assessment
Give a brief introduction to the survey on handout 3–A, "Parish Youth Ministry—Where Does It Stand?" and then administer it. After the participants have finished the survey, collect the papers and react to the responses, trying to project a picture of holistic and total youth ministry.

Brainstorming Session
1. Ask the participants this question and have them respond in writing, putting each dream on a separate sheet of paper: *If there were no limits, what would you like to see happening for the young people of this parish three years from now?*
2. After sufficient time, have them post their responses on the wall under these four categories: Programs, Personnel, Resources, and Other.
3. Invite the people to walk around and read the responses. Summarize what the people have hoped for, focusing on the Programs category.
4. Next focus on personnel and resources. Have the participants call out their responses to this question as you list them on newsprint: *What types of resources does your parish and local community already have that would help you make your dreams come true in three years' time?*
5. Then ask them to call out their responses to this question: *What problems or roadblocks would your parish have to overcome to achieve your dreams?* Write their responses on the newsprint.

Summary Evaluation
Summarize the main points of the meeting. Then let each member briefly share her or his feelings, attitudes, and comments about the way the meeting proceeded. Close the meeting with a prayer.

Survey
Parish Youth Ministry—Where Does It Stand?

This survey is designed to assess parish youth ministry. Read each item carefully and circle your response.

1. Overall, this is how I would rate our parish youth program:

   Very poor   Poor   Adequate   Good   Excellent

2. Our youth ministry program provides a good variety of religious education (catechetical) experiences.

   Strongly agree   Agree   Disagree   Strongly disagree   No opinion

3. If our youth ministry program needs more financial support in order to continue or improve, members of the parish are willing to provide it.

   Strongly agree   Agree   Disagree   Strongly disagree   No opinion

4. The training of catechists and youth workers in our program is effective and adequate.

   Strongly agree   Agree   Disagree   Strongly disagree   No opinion

5. Young people should be consulted about youth ministry activities.

   Strongly agree   Agree   Disagree   Strongly disagree   No opinion

6. Parents should be consulted about youth ministry activities.

   Strongly agree   Agree   Disagree   Strongly disagree   No opinion

7. Our confirmation preparation program clearly prepares our young people to take responsibility for their own faith.

   Strongly agree   Agree   Disagree   Strongly disagree   No opinion

8. Our confirmation program clearly prepares our young people to take responsibility for their membership in the Catholic church.

   Strongly agree   Agree   Disagree   Strongly disagree   No opinion

9. Our high school religious education offerings are responsive to the needs of our young people.

   Strongly agree   Agree   Disagree   Strongly disagree   No opinion

10. Our parish youth ministry program takes advantage of opportunities available on a regional level.

    Strongly agree   Agree   Disagree   Strongly disagree   No opinion

11. Our parish youth ministry program takes advantage of opportunities available on a diocesan level.

Strongly agree   Agree   Disagree   Strongly disagree   No opinion

12. Our parish youth ministry program includes adequate early adolescent (junior high) programming.

Strongly agree   Agree   Disagree   Strongly disagree   No opinion

13. The parish youth ministry program is a vital part of parish life.

Strongly agree   Agree   Disagree   Strongly disagree   No opinion

14. In-service, training, and educational experiences meet my needs for my role in youth ministry.

Strongly agree   Agree   Disagree   Strongly disagree   No opinion

15. I have attended in-service, training, or educational programs.

Yes   No

List those attended:

16. There is a written mission statement for youth ministry in my parish.

Yes   No   I don't know

17. There is a written statement of goals and objectives for the youth ministry program.

Yes   No   I don't know

18. Youth programs in my parish provide for meeting with the young people on a regular basis.

Yes   No   I don't know

19. My parish has an organized religious education program.

Yes   No   I don't know

20. Learning objectives are clearly identified for each of the religious education courses offered.

Yes   No   I don't know

21. Catechists and youth workers are provided with a variety of opportunities to learn and grow.

Yes   No   I don't know

22. Retreats are offered to the young people in my parish.

eighth and ninth grade: Yes   No   I don't know
tenth grade: Yes   No   I don't know
eleventh grade: Yes   No   I don't know
twelfth grade: Yes   No   I don't know

23. If retreats are offered, the young people of the parish attend them.

Yes   No   I don't know

24. There is an ongoing evaluation of the strengths and weaknesses of the youth ministry program for the parish.

Yes   No   I don't know

25. Additional comments:

CHAPTER 4

The Youth Ministry Commission

Questions for Reflection

- Does your parish have a mission statement that guides the pastoral ministry that takes place? Does the mission statement call for a ministry to youth?
- Draw a diagram of the various structures in your parish. How effectively do those structures relate to one another?
- How is youth ministry connected to the governing bodies in your parish?

What Is a Youth Ministry Commission?

The last chapter looked at the framework and work force for total youth ministry in a parish. With this picture in mind, I now want to focus on the piece of the framework—the youth ministry commission—that links a youth ministry work force to the parish and creates the kind of parish support that enables a total youth ministry effort.

No doubt youth ministry commissions will grow up in different forms and shapes in different parishes, but by describing my model I hope to point out the essential characteristics and purposes that make them what they are intended to be.

A youth ministry commission is a group of young people and adults who are representative of the parish. The group should have between five and nine members (although three or four might be adequate in a small parish).

The commission's primary purpose is to ensure that total youth ministry is vitally rooted in the parish and is seen by the parish as an integral part of its life and mission. In terms of its character, a youth ministry commission best models the concept of "servant leadership" as described by Robert Greenleaf, who says, "[Those who are led] will freely respond only to individuals who are chosen as leaders because they are proven and trusted as servants" (*Servant Leadership* [New York: Paulist Press, 1977], p. 10).

Why Is a Youth Ministry Commission Important?

The establishment of a youth ministry commission is vital to youth ministry because it ensures that pastoral care for young people is rooted in and supported by the whole parish. For much too long, the good work done for young people in parishes has been based on the vision, motivation, and energy of an individual or a small group of leaders—who often get burned out and quit or move on. A youth ministry commission, on the other hand, can establish parishwide ownership and responsibility that not only spreads out the work load and increases the level of energy but also carries on when key personnel move on.

What Does a Youth Ministry Commission Do?

In general the youth ministry commission functions as a vehicle through which the parish maintains ownership of its youth ministry and adequately provides for its operation. The more particular functions are those that follow:

Develops a mission statement for parish youth ministry: For dreams to come true they must have some foundation in reality. The commission provides this foundation for youth ministry by way of a mission statement, which documents the intention and conviction of the parish to provide youth ministry. It also answers the question of what youth ministry in the parish is to be, why the parish provides pastoral ministry to young people, what the parish believes regarding young people, who the constituents to be served are, and what is to be accomplished through the ministry. For example:

> We believe that by their baptism, young people in [your parish] are called to full membership in our church and to share their gifts and talents with other members, both now and as future leaders.
> In light of this belief, we see youth ministry as a vital part of the overall pastoral ministry offered by [your parish]. Through youth ministry we intend to meet the needs of young people in accord with their status.
> Meeting these needs means the following:
> * providing opportunities for faith formation and development of the total person: intellectually, emotionally, physically, and spiritually
> * developing relationships and sharing leadership between adults and young people
> * affirming the goodness of each person involved
> The range of young people to be served by youth ministry is young adolescents to young adults. Youth ministry at [your parish] will also serve parents and families of the young people and reach out to young people of other faiths and to those in the local community.

(See also appendix F, "Developing a Youth Ministry Mission Statement.")

Writes a constitution and bylaws: It is recommended that one bylaw stipulate that *Robert's Rules of Order* be used as a guide for conducting the business of the commission. The constitution should include the following:

The name of the commission

The commission's function and purpose: This should be drawn up in light of the mission statement. Include the lines of accountability to other agencies in the parish.

Membership: State the number of members and who they will represent. Name the pastor as an ex officio member and as one who ratifies decisions. The youth ministry coordinator is also an ex officio member and acts as the administrative officer of the commission. State the process by which commission members are chosen and include the length of term.

Leadership: Identify leadership roles such as chairperson, secretary, and so on, along with their functions.

Meetings: State the number of meetings and the regular schedule for them. Provide for ad hoc meetings. Indicate that unless otherwise noted, all meetings are open to the public.

Decision-making process: A consensus-seeking process is recommended. (See appendix G, "Using a Consensus-Seeking Process.")

Does long-range planning: As human beings we tend to be creatures of habit. If we do something once and it works, we tend to do it the same way again . . . and again . . . and again. Long-range youth ministry planning is essential to ensure that the changing needs of young people are being met, and it is especially important during these times of rapid change. A long-range planning process guarantees that a parish youth ministry program continually moves forward. A process for long-range planning will be given in chapter 5.

Establishes a budget: Far too often, getting money for the youth ministry program feels a lot like being sixteen years old again and asking Mom or Dad for the keys to the car.

The youth ministry commission can determine and request a budget that is seen as a request from the whole parish rather than from one person. Handout 4–A, "Budgeting for Youth Ministry," is a resource for putting together a budget for youth ministry. It is important for the commission to ensure that the young people are given opportunities to help plan the budget and raise some of the money for it.

Advocates for young people: Youth advocacy means taking a stand on behalf of young people when and where they do not have a voice, first to the church itself, and second to the wider society. It also means coaching and enabling young people to speak out when and where they do have recognized forums to do so. Further, advocacy includes speaking to young people on behalf of other young people when an injustice has occurred.

In light of the high percentage of young people who say they do not feel welcomed or accepted in the Catholic church, youth advocacy becomes a high priority of a youth ministry commission. Much of the hostile attitude young people find in a parish comes from generalized, often mistaken, negative images.

Finding examples of teenagers being the scapegoats for anything "bad" that happens in a parish is easy. Such an example occurred in a parish where I worked. There had been some minor damage to a door in the parish activities building. Immediately, the teenagers were accused and judged guilty. The sentence was that the activities facilities could not be used for any youth function for the following four months. There was no evidence produced, no jury, not even a trial . . . just a swift verdict and penalty. In fact, the teenagers had nothing to do with the damage that had occurred. A strong advocacy program that recognizes and publicizes what young people actually contribute to the church might have preempted such a presumptuous judgment and punishment.

Prays for young people: One of the most important tasks of commission members is to pray continually for the well-being of the young people in the parish and for the pastoral ministry to them.

Forms policy: Good policies ensure good and consistent growth. The commission forms policies needed to enable youth ministry and recommends them to the pastoral council and the pastor, who then either reject them or approve and promulgate them. The commission should also write rules to ensure that the policies passed by the council are appropriately implemented. In the event there is no pastoral council, the commission could both make and promulgate youth ministry policies if delegated to do so by the pastor. In any event, it usually is best to work through the existing system, thereby getting the youth ministry policies firmly rooted in the parish structure.

Recruits volunteers: No one person, or even several, can provide for all the various activities that constitute total youth ministry in a parish. The diverse needs of young people require the diverse knowledge, talents, and modeling of a broad spectrum of people. The youth ministry commission, with its representative membership, is in a good position to effectively help recruit and support volunteers who minister to the needs of young people.

Hires personnel: If a parish has one or more paid staff positions whose responsibilities include coordination of youth ministry, the commission would normally be the agent for formulating the job descriptions, doing the candidate searches and interviews, making recommendations for hiring, and carrying out contract negotiations. This process is described in chapter 6.

Provides support: Support is saying to people that you appreciate the work they do and value the contribution of their gifts and talents to ministry. It is an affirmation of the good work being done. The commission can express support to youth ministry volunteers and workers in many ways. For example, send cards on birthdays or anniversaries or at Christmas and Easter; send thank-you notes when an activity, event, or program is done well; sponsor a dinner at the end of the year. Support is also demonstrated through commissioning and recognition ceremonies at parish liturgies.

Support is especially important during times of crisis in the personal lives of youth ministers, such as illness or death in the family, or during times of crisis in the experience of the ministry itself, such as vandalism during a retreat. The commission can be the agent of support that keeps things in perspective so crises in youth ministry do not block out all the good that is done.

Evaluates youth ministry personnel and efforts: A positive evaluation process is an effective way to both maintain and support personnel who are accountable by contract. If the youth ministry commission is the hiring agent for youth ministry personnel, the commission should do these evaluations or make sure that the appropriate person or persons carry them out.

Likewise, the youth ministry commission should make sure that every program and event has an evaluation process built into it.

Also, the overall efforts of total youth ministry should be evaluated on an annual basis. This is a good way to monitor whether the ministry is meeting the needs of the young people in the parish.

Provides accountability to the parish's governing bodies: Being accountable is not only a responsibility of those entrusted with delegated authority but also a good way to maintain trust and support for efforts being made. A monthly report from the youth ministry commission on issues, concerns, activities, and events in parish youth ministry should be a regular part of the pastoral council meeting.

Situating a Youth Ministry Commission in the Parish Structure

One of the things I have learned from my meetings with parishes is that they are all different, and their structures are shaped and formed by many variables: staff, facilities, resources, finances, parish size, number of young people, parish mission statement, and so on. How a parish and its pastoral leaders choose to organize and administer the parish depends on these variables.

Let's take a look at where a youth ministry commission is best located among other parish bodies and draw some lines of communication and accountability. (This discussion presumes that the parish's governing body is made up of a pastor or parish administrator and a pastoral council or its equivalent.)

Structural location: Ideally the youth ministry commission is the connecting point between youth ministry and the pastoral council (see figure 7).

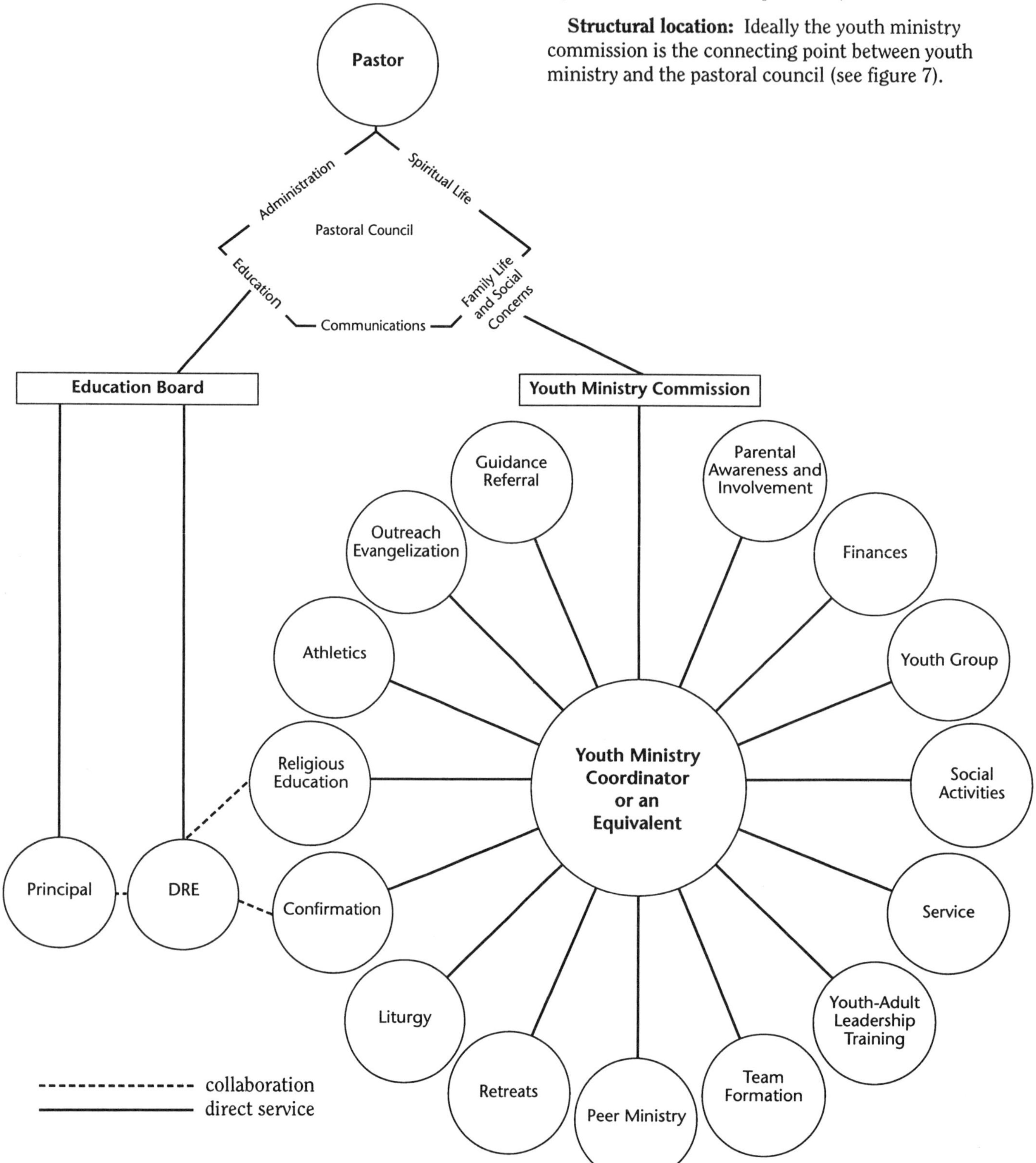

Figure 7. Structure of a Parish with a Youth Ministry Commision

Relationship with the pastor: The canonical authority for the entire parish pastoral ministry comes from the bishop through the pastor. The pastor does not have to be, and indeed should not be, the one who does all the ministries. However, the pastor does need to be regarded as the one who is responsible to the bishop for overseeing the ministries. Consequently, the youth ministry commission needs to make sure that the pastor is fully informed and given an account of all aspects of youth ministry. Again, when a commission operates in this fashion, the youth ministry efforts benefit from an added bonding to the entire pastoral ministry of a parish and an increased sense of parish ownership.

Relationship with the pastoral council: The parish pastoral council is by church law (canon 536) a consultative body that works in a collaborative relationship with the pastor. Consequently, the youth ministry commission normally relates with the pastor within the context of the pastoral council. It is important to be aware of the given purposes and roles of the pastoral council so that the youth ministry commission does not preempt what should properly be the function of the pastoral council. A sample list of a council's functions follows:

- prayerfully discerns the needs of the parish community
- serves as a vehicle for constructive dialog within the parish community
- identifies and calls forth the gifts and talents of the members of the parish community
- serves as a consultative body to the pastor
- develops a parish mission statement and plans for its implementation
- establishes clear and concise goals and objectives based on the parish mission statement and the emerging needs and concerns of the parish community
- ensures the implementation of parish goals and objectives by coordinating parish activities
- studies the needs and priorities of the diocesan church
- implements any policies of the diocese

Relationships with the parish school board, the parish board of religious education, and the parish administrator of religious education: Historically, Catholic schools and parish religious education programs (CCD) developed separately from, and sometimes prior to, youth ministry programs. Consequently, many parishes have well-established boards for schools and for parish religious education. These boards and their administrators are responsible for the formal and systematic religious education of young people in their faith formation. Some of the components of total youth ministry, such as confirmation preparation and the systematic catechesis called for by the Challenge document, have traditionally been and may still be the direct responsibility of these boards and administrators. If this is the case, the youth ministry commission needs to establish clear lines of accountability and communication with them and collaborate with them in these areas specific to educational formation.

The national thrust in youth ministry is to establish a unified youth ministry program that contains a religious education component, rather than running parallel youth ministry and religious education programs. To do this, the boards, the administrators, and the youth ministry commission should work together to present one program for young people—a program that integrates the educational component within the framework of total youth ministry. (An excellent resource for integrating religious education with youth ministry is *Ministries Growing Together,* by Kenneth Gleason et al.)

Relationships with the youth ministry coordinator, youth ministry leadership teams, activity leaders, and program volunteers: If a youth ministry coordinator preexists the establishment of a youth ministry commission, there may be need to redirect the coordinator's accountability from the board of education or the pastoral council to the youth ministry commission. If there is no parish coordinator, the commission should advocate for establishing the position and be the agent for hiring or appointing one.

Ideally, the youth ministry commission relates with leadership teams and activity leaders through the coordinator. If there is no overall coordinator, the commission must relate to them directly. This in effect makes the commission the coordinator of youth ministry. This is not a good arrangement and should be temporary at best.

Establishing a Youth Ministry Commission

Having described what a youth ministry commission is, how it fits into the parish structure, and how valuable it is to youth ministry and to the parish as a whole, let's move on to the task of establishing one.

The task is not an easy one and requires a lot of work. Oftentimes, parish leaders are resistant: "Why in the world do we need another committee?" "We can't find enough people to do what we already are doing, and you want more?" Do not let these put-offs dissuade you. The key to getting people involved is asking the right people, in the right way, to do something they will enjoy and are good at, for a reasonable amount of time.

If potential members know they will have adequate training, support, and supervision, putting together a commission can be most manageable. Do not get discouraged. A parish in southern Indiana worked for three years convincing parish leaders of the need for a youth ministry commission. They finally were convinced, and the results have been worth every effort.

Ideally, a task force for establishing a youth ministry commission should be appointed by the pastor or the pastoral council to carry out the steps described here. This not only takes care of steps 1 and 2 but also gives the new youth ministry commission a solid beginning as part of the parish's pastoral ministry.

1. Gain the support of the pastor. Realize that canonically the pastor is responsible for the administration of the parish and all pastoral ministries. Although the pastor does not necessarily have to be included in all the groundwork needed for establishing a commission, he needs to be informed and supportive of all that is done.

2. Gain the support of the pastoral council. By church law, the pastoral council consults and collaborates with the pastor in pastoral responsibilities. If you have a pastoral council, it must sanction the establishment of a commission.

3. Prepare job descriptions for commission members. If parishioners are to be effective in parish leadership roles, they need a clear idea of what they are expected to do. Job descriptions should be formulated for both adult and youth members of the commission. (See sample 4–A, "Job Descriptions for Members of a Youth Ministry Commission.")

4. Prepare procedures for selecting commission members. Three models for selecting commission members are described in appendix H. I recommend that the terms for commission members be staggered; that is, to start, commission members would have one-, two-, and three-year terms, with three-year terms becoming the norm after that.

5. Commission the commission members. The commission members should be announced to the community and commissioned as part of the structure of the parish. A commissioning ceremony led by the pastor, and perhaps involving parish council members, is an important affirmation of the role this group will play. Commissioning is best done at an appropriate parish liturgy.

6. Provide for commission members' initial education and formation. The most important initial task of the commission is to acquire an understanding of total youth ministry and how the commission serves to root it in the overall life of the parish. Have the new members read this chapter. Then schedule a two- to three-hour training session with them. A training session for new members of a youth ministry commission could proceed as follows:

Opening prayer: Begin the session with a prayer that allows for reflection and sharing on the purpose and intent of the training session.

Review quiz: Use the quiz on handout 4–B, "Youth Ministry—What Do You Know?" This is a fun, effective way to review the role and work of the commission.

Problem-solving exercise: One of the commission's most frequent tasks will be solving problems in the parish youth ministry program. Use handout 4–C, "Problem-Solving Scenarios," to practice this skill with your new commission members. (To shorten the session, use only two of the scenarios.)

Closing: Evaluate the session and close with a group prayer.

Providing for Ongoing Education and Formation

Ongoing education and formation for the youth ministry commission consists of opportunities for members to deepen their understanding of pastoral ministry in general and youth ministry in particular, along with an understanding of their unique role at both levels.

Ongoing education and formation can take place in various ways. Here are a few of the most possible opportunities that might be offered:

- Spend some time sharing hopes, dreams, fears, and concerns about young people in the parish.
- Read articles or view videos that deal with what is happening in young people's lives and what their concerns are.
- Read and discuss the first chapter of this book.
- Study and discuss *A Vision of Youth Ministry* and *The Challenge of Adolescent Catechesis.*
- Discuss the topic of servant leadership.
- Develop a youth ministry mission statement (see appendix F and the example on page 36). If a mission statement has already been formulated, discuss and reflect on it: What are the implications of this mission statement? What needs to be done to put it into effect? Is it practical? Is it realistic? Does it fit into the picture of pastoral ministry in our parish? Does it need revision or updating?
- If the commission does not already have a constitution and bylaws, then draft them.
- Read the book *All Grown Up and No Place to Go,* by David Elkind. It paints an incredibly vivid picture of where young people are. Discuss the book. Another book written by Elkind is *The Hurried Child.* It provides a great sketch of what is happening in the lives of young people.
- Give commission members opportunities to attend any available personal-growth, faith-formation, or leadership-development workshops that might fit the commission's needs and interests. Many are offered on diocesan, regional, and national levels.

- Hold a day of reflection, recreation, or relaxation together. Spend some time in prayer and discussion.
- Provide a formal training program. The manual *Training Adults for Youth Ministry,* by Robert McCarty and Lynn Tooma, contains excellent tools for training commission members.
- Participate in youth ministry accreditation programs. These can provide a good picture of what areas a commission needs to grow in.
- Encourage one another to keep dreaming. Do not be locked into the past. The lives of teenagers are changing every minute of every day. . . . Try to be that flexible!

Planning the Annual Calendar and Agendas

After establishing several youth ministry commissions and piloting them in parishes, I realized that a new commission needs clear and concrete direction. Often new commission members are concerned about "doing something," but a youth ministry commission's work tends to be more philosophical in nature. The commission's work is not as tangible or measurable as planning a retreat or teaching a confirmation class.

Meetings need to be well organized and have specific, clear agendas. (See the hints for holding meaningful meetings that are given in chapter 7.) Setting an agenda for each meeting not only helps the members get ready for the meeting but also facilitates the meeting and makes it effective. The following example shows a typical agenda for a youth ministry commission meeting, with comments on each agenda item:

1. Introductions and personal updates: Introductions are especially important if the participants do not know one another. A good way to put people at ease is to have them state their name, what school they are from or what they do for a living, and some interesting or seasonal question. For example, you might ask, What's your hobby? What's the best Christmas gift that you were able to give and why? or at Thanksgiving, What are you thankful for?

2. Opening prayer: The opening prayer should be more than just a short rote prayer. It should set the tone for the meeting. The members are encouraged to share in the prayer by helping to prepare it and by sharing spontaneous petitions during it.

3. Chairperson's opening remarks: The chairperson should open the meeting and take care of any leadership business, such as minutes for approval.

4. Decisions to be made: The first items of business should be those about which decisions need to be made at the meeting. These items should be addressed early on in the meeting so that the group has the energy to make good, informed decisions.

5. Impending decisions: This time can be used to hear further information about issues on which a decision will have to be made in the future.

6. Information or reports: This time is for committees or individuals to share information and reports other than those shared under items 4 and 5.

7. Summary and assignments: The chairperson can use this opportunity to summarize the main points of the meeting, to make any assignments.

8. Evaluation: Each member should have an opportunity to briefly share her or his feelings, attitudes, and comments about the way the meeting proceeded.

9. Closing prayer: Close the meeting with a short prayer of thanksgiving.

Also available for your reference in this book is a calendar of tasks for youth ministry commission meetings. Use it as a guideline for setting your own concrete agendas. (See appendix I, "An Annual Calendar of Tasks for a Youth Ministry Commission.") The calendar also suggests the kind of committees the commission will need to establish in order to carry out the commission's work. The usual procedure is for an executive committee to discuss the agenda before the commission meeting and then to make sure that all the information necessary for action is available at the meeting. Although each commission will be different because of the distinct nature of each parish, these agenda items and committees are common to most commissions.

Budgeting for Youth Ministry

In preparing your youth ministry budget, use the first two columns below for figures that you already know—the previous year's budgeted and actual income and expenses. With those figures as a guideline, enter proposed figures for your new budget.

Income	Budgeted	Actual	Proposed
Fund-raising			
Program Fees			
Donations			
Parish Subsidy			
Other			
Total			

Operating Expenses			
Salaries			
FICA, Retirement, Insurance			
Administrative Supplies			
Professional Enrichment			
Transportation Allowance			
Program Costs			
Resources, Equipment			
Stipends			
Other			
Total			

Job Descriptions for Members of a Youth Ministry Commission

Adult Members of a Youth Ministry Commission

Tasks and Involvement
- Attend youth ministry commission meetings
- Serve on commission committees as needed
- Be actively involved in the functions of the youth ministry commission, such as advocacy, long-range planning, budget formation, and support
- Serve as chairperson of the commission if chosen
- Serve as the commission's representative to the pastoral council if chosen

Qualifications
- Genuine care for young people and the lives of teenagers today
- Ability to communicate with young people and adults
- Dedication and commitment to the term of service
- Willingness to gain an understanding of teen culture

Accountability
The membership of the youth ministry commission is accountable to the pastor and the parish pastoral council.

Training
Members are expected to take part in the education, training, and formation of commission members provided during the regular commission meetings.

Benefits
- Impact on the quality of parish youth programs
- Positive influence in the lives of young people
- Ability to use gifts and talents that benefit the life and mission of ministry in the parish

Length of Commitment
Three years, from [month and year] to [month and year]

Youth Members of a Youth Ministry Commission

Tasks and Involvement
- Attend youth ministry commission meetings
- Serve on commission committees as needed
- Be actively involved in the functions of the youth ministry commission, such as advocacy, long-range planning, budget formation, and support

Qualifications
- Care for peers
- Willingness to learn about the concept of total youth ministry
- Ability to relate to peers and adults
- Dedication and commitment to the term of service

Accountability
The membership of the youth ministry commission is accountable to the pastor and the parish pastoral council.

Training
Members are expected to take part in the education, training, and formation of commission members provided during the regular commission meetings.

Benefits
- Impact on the quality of parish youth programs
- Positive influence in the lives of peers
- Ability to use gifts and talents that benefit the life and mission of ministry in the parish

Length of Commitment
One year, from [month and year] to [month and year]

Quiz
Youth Ministry—What Do You Know?

This quiz is intended to be a discussion starter on the role and work of the parish youth ministry commission. Complete the quiz, and then we will discuss the expected answers as a group.

True or False

_____ 1. A youth ministry commission is a body of young people.

_____ 2. A commission should have at least twenty-four members to be effective.

_____ 3. *"Total" youth ministry* is a term that is in vogue, so that young people can relate to it as "totally awesome"!

_____ 4. The establishment of a commission is vital to a parish that wants to do intentional, effective ministry to young people.

_____ 5. A holistic approach to youth ministry includes early and older adolescents (junior high and high school) and young adults.

_____ 6. A commission gives the parish a sense of ownership in providing for the needs and concerns of its young people.

_____ 7. A parish should hire a youth minister to minister to all the needs of all the young people.

_____ 8. "Visioning" and "long-range planning" refer to having your eyes checked sometime in the next three years.

_____ 9. Youth ministry team members (the planners, the activity organizers, and so on) are the "doers" and the "movers and shakers" of the program.

_____ 10. Whatever you do, make sure that the pastor is the last to know what is going on. He does not have to worry about things then.

Multiple Choice
For each statement, circle the letter or letters that accurately complete the sentence.

1. *Pastoral ministry* is a term that refers to
   a. small-group sharing in a cow pasture
   b. dealing with people and their needs, not just programs
   c. Louis Pasteur, after whom it is named
   d. a part of the ministry of our church

2. The pastoral council is
   a. a committee of pastors
   b. a new rock band
   c. a consultative, collaborative body to guide the parish
   d. none of the above

3. The board of education
   a. is a paddle used in schools to spank children who misbehave
   b. is a group to be tolerated
   c. can be bought at the local lumberyard
   d. is responsible for religious education in the parish

4. In the parish structure, a youth ministry commission is most effectively placed
   a. under the board of education
   b. in the gym
   c. under the pastoral council
   d. directly accountable to no one

5. The functions of a youth ministry commission include
   a. budget formation
   b. youth advocacy
   c. support of youth ministry
   d. policy recommendation
   e. evaluation of events
   f. hiring recommendations
   g. reporting to the pastoral council
   h. long-range planning
   i. all of the above
   j. none of the above

6. Religious education
   a. refers to the learning styles of priests and nuns
   b. is a more appropriate term than CCD
   c. is most effective in the context of total youth ministry
   d. is lifelong
   e. has nothing to do with young people
   f. all of the above

7. Formation and education of a commission
   a. is ongoing
   b. should be part of each meeting
   c. refers to the amount of schooling the members have
   d. should be done for all the parish as well

8. A commission task force is
   a. a group of commission members designated as problem solvers
   b. a group of parents on the commission who make young people do something they do not want to do
   c. a group appointed to do preliminary work in establishing a commission
   d. ideally appointed by the pastoral council

9. To become a member of a commission you should be
   a. initially appointed
   b. made to do it
   c. elected by the parish
   d. someone who cares for young people
   e. willing to work on youth programs

Answers
When photocopying the quiz, be sure to block out this section of answers.

True or False
1. false (body of young people and adults)
2. false (five to nine members)
3. false (*Total* means comprehensive.)
4. true
5. true
6. true
7. false (to coordinate various youth ministry activities)
8. false (planning for the future)
9. false (Activity leaders and program volunteers are the "doers" and the "movers and shakers" of the program.)
10. false (Make sure he knows what is going on.)

Multiple Choice
1. b, d
2. c
3. d
4. c
5. i
6. b, c, d
7. a, b, d
8. c, d
9. a, c, d

Problem-Solving Scenarios

Cut this handout along the dotted lines to form four slips of paper.

Scenario 1: Your parish board of education has told the youth group leaders that too many activities are going on and that youth group members cannot manage to go to everything. They ask that some things be cut. In fact, they have asked that the car wash scheduled for next weekend be canceled. Needless to say, the organizers of the car wash are not happy and have placed the issue on the agenda for your commission meeting. How would you deal with this as a commission? What would be your response?

Scenario 2: Last year, several teenagers were suspected of drug abuse, including alcohol consumption at the parish lock-in. This has generated some heated discussions at a couple of youth group meetings, about how to respond to such behavior. Consequently, your youth ministry coordinator has asked the commission to develop a policy on what to do about young people who abuse illegal substances at parish youth activities. As a group, how would you go about developing such a policy? What would it be?

Scenario 3: A formation and education committee was appointed from the commission to plan activities and bring to each meeting ideas for education and formation of the commission members. Several months have gone by and no ideas or opportunities have been presented at the meetings. The commission leaders have placed this concern on the agenda. How would you deal with it and why?

Scenario 4: Rumor has it that several members of the parish pastoral council have complained that money is being wasted on the youth ministry coordinator's salary. After all, there are plenty of good volunteers who could do the job. As a commission, what would be your response and why?

PART C

The Planning and Maintaining of Parish Youth Ministry

CHAPTER 5

Long-range Planning

Questions for Reflection

- If you were to grade your parish's youth ministry effort, what grade would you give? Why?
- What are some of the things you would like to see the parish do for young people that have not been done in the past?
- Does your daily work planning look to the achievement of longer-range goals?
- What do you foresee as being the most difficult aspect of long-range planning for youth ministry?

The Need for Long-range Planning

The rapid changes that have affected and continue to affect youth ministry make it critical that a parish have a planning process that can keep up. The bishops of the Second Vatican Council tell us:

The accelerated pace of history is such that one can scarcely keep abreast of it. The destiny of the human race is viewed as a complete whole, no longer, as it were, in the particular histories of various peoples: now it merges into a complete whole. And so mankind substitutes a dynamic and more evolutionary concept of nature for a static one, and the result is an immense series of new problems calling for a new endeavor of analysis and synthesis. (*The Church in the Modern World,* no. 5)

The challenge that the decree presents to the church at large likewise challenges leaders of youth ministry to plan in the face of change, using the best of human wisdom while recognizing that the mystery of God works within and beyond our plans.

A refresher on the benefits of good planning follows:
- Planning allows you to look at dreams and translate them into action.
- Planning points somewhere and then lays out a way to get there.
- Planning is decision-making in advance of action.
- Planning permits initiation and response rather than reaction.
- Planning provides an opportunity for a larger group of people to help shape decisions.
- Planning enables you to eliminate unnecessary duplication of effort, poor use of resources, or fragmented action.
- Planning provides a vision within which leaders can direct their service.
- Planning makes the work you do intentional rather than accidental.

Who Does Long-range Planning?

If the planning for youth ministry is to be rooted in the parish and to have a firm hope of being carried out, it is best done by a youth ministry commission (or an equivalent parish group)—a sort of mission control—that represents the whole parish. Planning for youth ministry is at its best when it is part of a comprehensive parish pastoral planning process. If your parish has this type of overall planning process in place, it will greatly facilitate long-range planning for youth ministry.

When planning for youth ministry, the youth ministry commission needs to work closely with the youth ministry coordinator (if there is one) and also with the pastor and the pastoral council. Regular communication with the pastor and the pastoral council during the planning process will aid in their understanding of the final plan once it is presented.

Appointing a commission planning committee is an effective strategy for planning. This committee both begins and completes the planning process. Its role is to gather information needed to initiate the planning process and then to ensure that all steps of planning are completed. The planning itself is done in conjunction with the commission and approved by it.

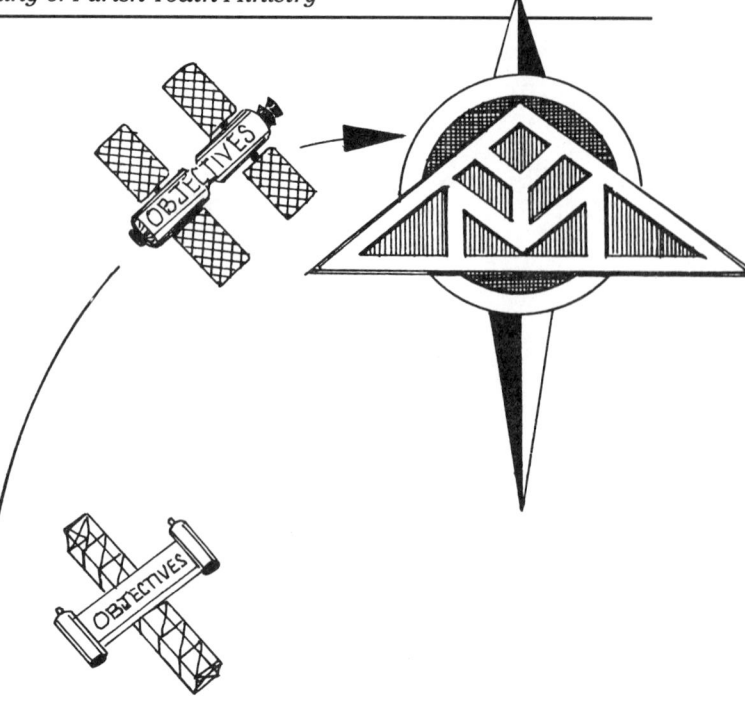

Figure 8. Long-range Planning for Youth Ministry

What Is Long-range Planning for Youth Ministry?

Long-range planning for youth ministry has two levels: *strategic planning*, which includes setting long-range goals, and *operational planning*, which includes setting annual objectives and designing action plans for specific events or activities.

Strategic and operational planning might be visualized in terms of a space shuttle launch. Youth ministry is the shuttle to be launched. The destination of the launch is the youth ministry mission of the parish. The youth ministry mission of the parish provides the direction and the purpose of the ministry. The long-range goals of strategic planning provide the trajectory of the launch, the path to be followed to the destination. The annual objectives of operational planning are the space stations, located along the trajectory, to be reached and to serve as checkpoints. The action plans of operational planning are the main-stage rocket that carries the youth ministry shuttle to its space stations along the trajectory, and to its final destination—the youth ministry mission of the parish.

The Components of Long-range Planning

Before going further into the planning process, it is important to define its primary components: *goals, objectives,* and *action plans* (these components will be further discussed in the context of planning as I go through the steps of strategic and operational planning).

Goals: Goals are broad, general statements that provide targets for youth ministry efforts and move youth ministry toward the accomplishment of its mission. They also provide a common purpose and cause for all persons involved in the youth ministry effort and define what is to be accomplished over the long term. In the three-year planning process used in my model, the goals are to be achieved at the end of three years.

Objectives: Objectives are statements that name specific and measurable outcomes that need to be accomplished to reach the goals. Each year's objectives during the course of a three-year plan move the effort closer to the goals that are expected to be reached at the end of three years.

Action plans: Action plans are specific details and schedules of activities and events that will accomplish the objectives for each year of the overall plan.

An example of planning that involves goals, objectives, and action plans might be helpful here. Suppose that there is a need to nurture in the young people a sense of belonging and connectedness to the parish. In response, the following three-year *goal* is set: *To have a place in the parish facilities for young people to come, have fun, socialize, and grow intellectually, emotionally, physically, and spiritually.*

The *objectives* to be accomplished to reach this goal might be as follows:

Year 1
- Determine if any space in the present physical facilities could be built into a youth center.
- Determine what design and facilities a youth center would need and what the cost might be.

Year 2
- Research the financial feasibility of building a parish youth center.
- Institute a plan to raise funds needed to build and equip a parish youth center.

Year 3
- Build and equip a parish youth center.

The *action plans* for the first objective of year 1 might be the following:
- A committee is appointed in August to work on the project.
- The committee interviews pastoral staff in September regarding the availability of space in the present physical facilities for a parish youth center.
- The committee contacts the pastoral council maintenance committee in September regarding space for a parish youth center.
- The committee reports their findings to the youth ministry commission in October.

Each *goal* will probably have a number of objectives that flow from it for each year. Each *objective* will probably have a specific set of *action plans* to accomplish the objective.

Specifics of the Planning Process

Any planning process is a series of steps that leads to decision-making and action. The following list shows the sequential steps of strategic and operational planning. Remember, as I noted in the introduction, this planning process is a thorough one, even idealistic. You may not be able to, or need to, follow every detail in the way it is given. However, it will provide a reliable guide for designing a planning process as well as a good measuring stick for evaluating an existing one. A suggested timetable that fits with a July-to-June planning year is included.

Strategic Planning Steps
1. Form a planning committee (September).
2. Hold a visioning experience, an opportunity to dream (October).
3. Develop a sense of mission (October).
4. Do an environmental scan of the parish and an assessment of current parish youth ministry efforts (November).
5. Analyze the data (December).
6. Set (or revise) long-range goals (January).

Operational Planning Steps
7. Develop annual objectives for accomplishing long-range goals (February).
8. Evaluate and refine proposed long-range goals and annual objectives (March).
9. Design action plans for carrying out annual objectives (April).
10. Begin implementation of action plans and continue evaluation (July).

As you read through the specifics of these planning steps, remember that steps 1 through 6 are the steps of strategic planning—the setting of long-range goals—and that steps 7 through 10 are the steps of operational planning—the establishing of more immediate objectives and action plans.

1. Form a Planning Committee (September)

The chairperson of the youth ministry commission appoints a planning committee in September. The committee can number anywhere from three to seven members and should include an adult member of the commission, a young person, and the youth ministry coordinator. An adult commission member best serves as chairperson of the committee and as the one who reports back to the commission about the committee's work.

Make sure to include members who are not on the commission. Look for people who have a gift for planning and organizing along with a sense of vision. Try to have a mix of ethnic groups and age-groups represented. In recruiting, it helps to tell prospective volunteers that the committee work is a short-term commitment and to explain what the expectations are. Developing a brief job description is an important and effective part of the recruitment process. An outline of a job description can be found in chapter 7, under the subhead "Provide Job Descriptions."

Once a planning committee is formed, its first meeting should be with the youth ministry commission, and the meeting should include an overview of the whole planning process as well as a time for prayer and sharing.

2. Hold a Visioning Experience (October)

The first assignment for the planning committee is to facilitate a visioning experience. Giving people a chance to dream allows them to unleash their creativity, unencumbered by obstacles that the analytical, technical, and data-based dimensions of planning often present.

The visioning experience can be provided in a number of formats. It can be done at different times with the different leadership groups in the parish such as the pastoral council, the parish staff, the commission itself, education boards, parent groups, and youth groups. Or it might be more efficient to gather a broad base of people in one meeting, making sure that the various groups are represented.

The story of a visioning experience is told in chapter 3. Chapter 3 also offers two resources on this: sample 3–A, "A Process for a Parish Visioning Experience," and handout 3–A, a survey titled "Parish Youth Ministry— Where Does It Stand?"

You can also use handout 3–A for gaining input from those who did not attend the visioning meeting. It can be administered at staff meetings, pastoral council meetings, youth gatherings, and the like. Or this handout can be done in a large-group situation like a liturgy. When such an instrument is given out in a group situation, allow time to complete it and return it right there. A mailing is another option. If it is mailed you might assign some people to a phone committee to follow up. They should be prepared to ask the questions that are on the instrument in order to get a substantial and authentic return.

3. Develop a Sense of Mission (October)

Once the planning committee has a grasp of what the parish is thinking and what it is willing to support, it is time to develop a sense of mission for the three-year effort. First find a copy of the most recent mission statement for youth ministry as well as the overall mission statement of the parish. Relate the findings of the visioning experience and the needs assessment instruments to these mission statements to see if they are compatible. If not, make recommendations for revisions to the commission and the pastoral council. If your parish does not have either of these mission statements, develop a mission statement for parish youth ministry. It should cover the following statements about youth ministry:

• We believe . . .
• We serve . . .
• Therefore we do . . .

Your statement may use different wording, but all in all, a youth ministry mission statement should be able to respond to any question about the purpose of youth ministry in the parish. For help with this process, see appendix F, "Developing a Youth Ministry Mission Statement."

4. Scan the Parish Environment and Assess Youth Ministry Efforts (November)

Step 4 requires a great deal of energy and effort in gathering the information needed to plan effectively for the future. Several important aspects of this information gathering process are described here.

The environmental scan: *Environment* in this context refers to the material and spiritual surroundings that affect the young people in the parish and any ministry to them. A scan of the environment helps determine whether it helps or hinders the youth ministry effort and can point out areas of the environment that call for special attention in planning youth ministry.

For example, youth ministry in a small-town parish located in a predominantly Protestant Bible Belt might call for special attention to scriptural study for the Catholic teenagers. This might help them feel more comfortable with their Protestant peers who might confront their Catholic beliefs by way of the Scriptures. Or a very different approach to ministry might be needed in a small parish that was once rural but now has large housing developments and youth from two very different backgrounds.

To carry out the environmental scan, have members of the planning committee select areas of the environment they wish to gather information on. Handout 5–A, "A Parish Environmental Scan," can help with this task.

The youth ministry assessment: The second task of information gathering is the youth ministry assessment, which has two parts. The first part is gathering information from the young people of the parish. The second part is gathering information from the parish staff and adults at large. The surveys on handouts 5–B and 5–C, "Parish Youth Ministry—Does It Work for You?" and "Parish Youth Ministry—How Do You See It?" respectively, can help with this task.

A good deal of assessment data may already have been collected at the visioning experience (if one was held). You might compare that data with the data called for on handout 5–A to determine what areas still need to be assessed.

Survey of young people: If another assessment of young people is called for, it can be done in a number of ways.

• Conduct personal interviews with focus questions. Members of the planning committee can each interview a specific number of young people, either by phone or in person. The focus questions can be drawn from handout 5–B.

- Hold a focus session at a youth gathering. Secure an agenda slot at a regularly scheduled gathering such as the parish youth group meeting and ask the members to fill out handout 5–B.

Survey of parish staff and the parish at large: You might use different methods for assessing the parish staff and the parish at large.
- Handout 5–C can be used to assess the parish staff.
- To assess the parish at large, use handout 5–C, or your own shortened version of it. Or use the survey on handout 5–D, "Youth Ministry—Tell Us What You Think." Either of these can be given out at liturgies.

A collated report of the results of the environmental scan and the youth ministry assessment should be drawn up by the planning committee.

5. Analyze the Data (December)

In this process, data analysis is a thorough and critical examination of the results of the youth ministry assessment and environmental scan. Rarely does raw data tell the whole story, but in light of analysis and discussion, the information can reveal a clear picture of what is going on. This picture will serve as a backdrop for establishing long-range goals when planning for a total youth ministry.

The analysis of data is best done at a joint meeting of the youth ministry commission, the youth ministry staff, and the planning committee. Handout 5–E, "Parish Data Analysis," can also help in this task.

Preparation for the data analysis meeting: The commission chairperson should arrange a meeting time (the meeting itself will take one and a half to two hours) and make the following preparations:
- Make available to all the meeting participants copies of the collated report of the environmental scan and youth ministry assessment. Have them review the report before the meeting and note areas of concern.
- Make available to all the participants copies of handout 5–E. Ask them to jot down on part A of this sheet areas of strengths, weaknesses, opportunities, and concerns that the report revealed.

Process for the data analysis meeting: Before the meeting begins, provide refreshments and an opportunity to relax.
- When the group is settled, the commission chairperson should offer an opening prayer asking for the guidance of the Holy Spirit, the gift of listening, and the courage to dream and share.
- Place on the wall four large sheets of newsprint with the following four headings: Strengths, Weaknesses, Opportunities, Concerns.

- Ask the members to list on the corresponding sheet of newsprint the strengths, weaknesses, opportunities, and concerns from their data analysis sheet. You might want to have several sheets for each heading so people can write and stay out of one another's way. Listing the data in this way amounts to categorizing the information into a manageable and logical arrangement.
- Allow the group to reflect on what has been written on the newsprint. Then open the floor for discussion to clarify and question the information that has surfaced. There is a good chance that the group will have generated more opportunities and concerns than can be responded to immediately. The strengths and weaknesses will help determine what should be done and what the parish is able to do. This process should reveal what is really possible before the goal-setting process begins.
- While retaining a reflective and prayerful mood, ask each member to jot on part B of the handout the top three strengths, weaknesses, opportunities, and concerns they have.
- Split the group into smaller groups of about three people each. Try to mix commission members, youth ministry staff members, and planning committee members in each group; put new members with veterans, and young people with older people.
- Assign the following tasks to the groups (allow about twenty to thirty minutes for these tasks): (1) Have the members of each group share their lists, one area at a time. (2) Choosing from all four areas, have each group identify and prioritize the top ten items they believe need to be addressed in a youth ministry effort. Write these in part C of the handout.
- Bring the small groups back together. Have each group post and explain its list of prioritized items. As an entire group, discuss and decide which items are the top priorities and require planning for the future. This information and discussion will provide the basis for setting the long-range goals needed to move youth ministry efforts into the future.

6. Set Long-range Goals (January)

Step 6 can be carried out as a second phase of a daylong meeting that began with step 5, the analysis of data. Or it can be a separate meeting that reconvenes those who were at the data analysis meeting.

Setting long-range goals is the final step in the strategic part of long-range planning, and it provides impetus and direction for the operational part of long-range planning. Remember, the goals determine the path to be followed to accomplish the mission.

The goals to be set are expected to be reached at the end of a three-year period, including the current year if this is the first time this process has been undertaken. Examples of long-range goals include the following:

- that the young people of the parish see the parish as a safe place to belong, where they can grow personally and spiritually
- that the parish provides for the physical, spiritual, and emotional well-being of younger and older adolescents as well as young adults of the parish

Process for long-range goal setting: Briefly explain the nature of long-range goals and then use the following process for setting them:

- Divide the group into small groups of three or four persons each. From the list of top priorities identified at the data analysis meeting, assign at least one item to each small group. If there are more items than small groups, some small groups may have to work with more than one item. Give each small group a copy of handout 5–F, "Goal Setting," for each assigned item.
- Taking one item at a time, ask each small group to answer the questions on handout 5–F. The answer to question 1 will result in a goal statement. Then have each group write the item and its goal statement on a large piece of newsprint to be posted for all to see. This activity should be completed in about thirty minutes.
- Have each group post and explain its item(s) and its goal(s). After each report, allow enough time for discussion, questions, and revisions in order to arrive at a consensus that the goal is an appropriate one.

7. Develop Objectives (February)

Once the long-range goals have been established, annual objectives for accomplishing the goals must be developed. This begins the operational part of long-range planning. If possible, the development of the objectives is also a part of the one-day planning process. Ideally the objectives should be developed by the same small group that developed the goals to which they are related. If there is a strong need first to have the goals formally approved by the youth ministry commission, the planning committee could develop the objectives rather than try to reassemble the whole goal-setting group.

Process for developing objectives: To prepare for this process, reproduce copies of handout 5–G, "A List of Verbs for Setting Objectives," blocking off the bottom of the sheet so handout 5–H does not show up.

- For each goal, have the small groups (or the planning committee) develop objectives for each of the three

years of the long-range plan. Remember that objectives are statements that name specific and measurable steps that need to be taken to accomplish the goal. Handout 5–G can be distributed to assist the small groups in this step.

- When objectives for each of the three years have been written for each goal, post them on newsprint for the whole group to read and discuss. State the goal at the top, next list the objectives for year one, then for year two, and then for year three. As with the goals, allow enough discussion and revision to arrive at a consensus that each objective is appropriate and consistent with its respective goal.
- At this point refer the goals and objectives to an editorial team to edit for formal presentation to the youth ministry commission at an appropriate time.

8. Evaluate Goals and Objectives (March)

The goals and objectives need to be approved by the youth ministry commission. Handout 5–H, "Evaluating Goals and Objectives," can be used for this. Then the proposed goals and objectives should be evaluated by the parish community at large. A report containing the following information should be prepared for carrying out the evaluation:

- youth ministry priorities
- the goals and objectives that were derived from these priorities
- a preface explaining long-range planning and what such planning is intended to accomplish

The people who will evaluate this report are parents, adults who work with young people, and the young people themselves.

There are several ways this evaluation can be carried out.

- Mail the report to the responders. If responses are to be mailed in, ask the respondents to write out any questions, comments, or suggestions, making them specific to each goal and objective.
- At a general gathering, perhaps a liturgy, distribute the report and receive the responses verbally.
- At a special evaluation meeting, you will have an opportunity to use a process for gathering responses. First, distribute the report. Then in small groups, have the people identify those goals and objectives that are questionable and make suggestions for their modification.

A report on the results of the evaluation should then be given to the youth ministry commission for the final refinement of the goals and objectives.

9. Design Action Plans (April)

Action plans are those programs, events, and activities selected for achieving the objectives.

Action plans are best prepared by those who will be responsible for carrying them out, that is, the youth ministry staff and volunteers. For example, if one of the goals and its objective is to develop skills and build self-esteem of young people through physical activities, the leadership team of that aspect of youth ministry, in this case, perhaps the team in charge of community building, would design the action plans. If the youth ministry structure is further divided so that athletics is an area that has a leadership team, these people would design the action plans.

Designing action plans actually takes place on two levels. *Level 1* is the identification of the kinds of programs, events, and activities needed to achieve the goals and objectives. At this stage, the feasibility of programs, events, or activities is considered in light of personnel and resources. *Level 2* is the drawing up of directions for the implementation of a program, event, or activity along with the scheduling, staffing, and resource provisions.

Before beginning to design action plans, be sure to consider any input the young people may have provided from their evaluation of previous programs, events, and activities.

Level 1 Planning

1. Write down the goal, and under it write the objective and the year it is to be achieved.
2. Write down the type of program, event, or activity that will best achieve the objective. Make sure that it is clear just what is to be done and that the personnel and the resources to do it are available.
3. Estimate how much it will cost.

Level 2 Planning

1. Determine when the program, event, or activity is to be carried out.
2. Write a detailed description of how the program, event, or activity is to be carried out.
3. Make a list of the tasks to be performed to carry out the action plan. Assign a time frame for doing these tasks.
4. Determine what qualities are needed in those who will carry out the tasks.
5. Develop job descriptions for those who will carry out the tasks.
6. Make provisions for recruiting, training, and supporting those who will carry out the tasks.
7. Make provisions for evaluating the program, event, or activity and those who carried it out.

The last four items in this process will be more fully detailed in chapter 7, "Building a Pool of Volunteers."

An important point here is that initially budget needs should flow from effective long-range planning rather than from availability of financial resources. Planning should guide the budget, not vice versa. On the other hand, the availability of financial resources will modify what actually is able to be done.

Initially, action plans are developed for year one of a three-year plan and are submitted to the youth commission for approval in the previous March. Implementation can then begin in July, the beginning of year one. Also, by January of year one, the commission will need to assign the designing of action plans for year two, almost six months before the beginning of year two in July. The same schedule is used for designing action plans for year three. (Note: The years in this model run from July 1 to June 30.)

A number of good resources have been published for designing the action plans, though their terminology may be different from mine. These resources are listed in the section "For Further Reading" at the end of this book.

10. Implement the Action Plans and Continue Evaluation (July)

Implementation of the action plans: The implementation of the action plans will be done by the youth ministry staff and volunteers. However, part of the planning process is to develop a calendar or schedule for the programs, events, and activities selected. The development of this calendar, like the designing of the actions plans, is best done by the youth ministry staff and volunteers. Sample 5–A, "A Youth Ministry Planning Schedule," shows what three months of a youth ministry schedule might look like.

Ongoing evaluation of the action plans: The purpose of ongoing evaluation of the action plans is twofold: first, to enable observation of the progress of the plan and its implementation, and second, to discover how plans might be modified and improved in the next planning cycle.

Programs, events, and activities are evaluated best right after they are held. Evaluation by the young people who participated in the event, program, or activity is particularly important. Simply ask them to give the experience a grade (A = great, B = good, C = fair, D = poor, and F = failing). Then ask two questions: What did you like best about the event? What could have been better?

Young people who participated in the overall youth ministry events for the year should also complete a year-end evaluation. (See sample 5–B, "An Evaluation of Youth Ministry Activities.") The youth ministry workers who staffed the events can follow the same evaluation procedure. Then the evaluations by staff and youth can be combined into an evaluation report and presented to the youth ministry commission. Such evaluations and reports could be done midyear, too, if not quarterly.

The youth ministry commission should review the

goals and objectives in light of the evaluation reports at least twice a year, if not quarterly. This review should answer the following questions:

• Has there been progress as planned?
• If there has not been progress, why not?
• What has been done well?
• Are the goals and objectives still realistic? Do they need to be modified?
• Are the resources allocated being used effectively and appropriately? Are there enough resources?
• What still needs to be done, given our timeline?

The youth ministry commission should do a comprehensive evaluation at the end of each fiscal year. It should include not only the previous questions but also a reflection on the total planning experience. The commission should ask itself if the planning process has been a good experience for them and if it has been positive in its outcomes for the young people of the parish and for the parish as a whole.

A written report of the year-end evaluation by the commission should be submitted to the pastoral council. A summary of the report should be shared with the youth ministry staff and volunteers, the young people and their parents, and the parish as a whole.

When the work of long-range planning is described all at once, it can seem to be an overwhelming task. But remember, it is spread out over a three-year period. And many of the tasks involved are tasks that are commonly carried out in a youth ministry effort anyway. It is just that here they are incorporated as part of a systematic planning process. The first year of planning is the critical year. It involves the most work and most meetings and sets the framework for planning in succeeding years.

The results of long-range planning are well worth the effort and work that they require. Done in good spirit, planning is a way of joining forces with the spirit of God so that our church might more effectively touch the lives, the hearts, and the souls of young people.

A Parish Environmental Scan

Determine which areas of the parish environment you wish to gather information on. Then fill in the pertinent sections of this worksheet. Helpful sources of information might be a library, the diocesan office, census data, the chamber of commerce, and so on.

Geographical Data
Describe the broad area served by the parish. Include boundaries, square mileage, a brief comment on the nature of the area (rural, urban, etc.), a list of communities, and significant physical features. Please note areas of change such as residential or commercial developments under way or planned.

_____

_____

_____

_____

Population Data
List various characteristics of the youth population served by the parish. Suggested measures include the following:

	10 years ago	Present	10 years projected
• Total youth population	_____	_____	_____
• Ethnic youth population			
Black	_____	_____	_____
Hispanic	_____	_____	_____
Asian	_____	_____	_____
Other	_____	_____	_____
• Age distribution			
10- to 14-year-olds	_____	_____	_____
15- to 18-year-olds	_____	_____	_____
19- to 30-year-olds	_____	_____	_____

Economic Data
Income levels: _____

Unemployment rate: _____

Poverty income level: _____

Major occupations for people in this area: _____

_____

Other economic data significant to this parish: _____

_____

_____

Family Life Data

Average size of families in this area: _____

Number of two-parent families: _____

Number of single-parent families: _____

Divorce rate: _____

Number of abused children: _____

Education Data

Number of schools in this area: _____

Number of public schools: _____

Total enrollment in public schools: _____

Number of parochial and private schools: _____

Total enrollment in
parochial and private schools: _____

Sources for adult education:

_____

_____

_____

_____

_____

Religion Data

Number of Catholics in this area: _____

Other denominations in this area:

_____

_____

Percentage of Catholics unchurched: _____

Religious issues that are dominant in this area:

_____

_____

Other ecumenical information significant to this

area: _____

_____

Financial Data

Number of envelope holders: _____

Number of active envelope users: _____

Annual parish income: _____

Annual parish expense: _____

Annual youth ministry budget: _____

Annual school budget: _____

Parish Membership Data

	10 years ago	Present	10 years projected
Total number of individuals	_____	_____	_____
Total number of households	_____	_____	_____
Number of families registered	_____	_____	_____
Number of families leaving	_____	_____	_____

Paid Pastoral Staff

Indicate the number of people in each of the following positions:

	10 years ago	Present	10 years projected
Priest	_____	_____	_____
Pastoral associate	_____	_____	_____
Director of religious education or coordinator of religious education	_____	_____	_____
Youth ministry coordinator	_____	_____	_____
Secretary	_____	_____	_____
Accountant	_____	_____	_____
Principal	_____	_____	_____
Teacher	_____	_____	_____
Physical plant manager and staff	_____	_____	_____
Music director	_____	_____	_____
Other	_____	_____	_____

Survey

Parish Youth Ministry—Does It Work for You?

In the first column, list all the parish youth ministry activities and programs, including religious education and confirmation, that you participate in. Then for each one respond to the questions in the following columns.

Check your age-group:
_____ 10- to 14-year-olds
_____ 15- to 18-year-olds

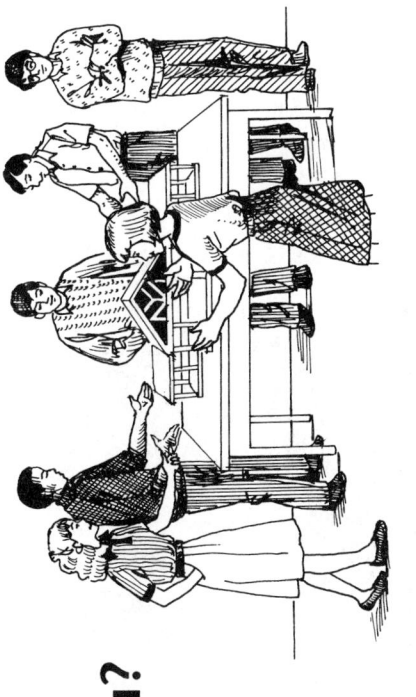

Programs and Activities	Is the program or activity filling a need that young people have?	Were young people part of the decision-making and planning process for this program or activity?	List needs that this program or activity fills.	Is this program or activity scheduled on a regular basis?	Do the meeting times fit your schedule?	Do an adequate number of adults participate in the program or activity?
1.						
2.						
3.						
4.						
5.						
6.						
7.						
8.						

Survey

Parish Youth Ministry—How Do You See It?

The Youth Ministry Program

1. Are the programs and activities holistic and comprehensive? _____

2. How are youth needs determined?

   _____

   _____

3. What programs and activities are being offered to meet the needs of young people?

   _____

   _____

4. Are parents and families being included in programs and events in order to meet their needs? _____

5. Is religious education part of the parish's total youth ministry? _____

6. What kind of teaching methods are being used in religious education?

   _____

   _____

7. Are clear objectives set for the religious education program? _____

8. Is a systematic approach used in the religious education program? _____

9. Are retreat opportunities available? _____

10. Are there opportunities for young people to share their gifts with the church and community through service? _____

11. Are leadership training programs offered to enable the young people and adults to develop their gifts? _____

12. Is progress in youth ministry programs reported to the young people? to the parents? How?

    _____

    _____

Administration and Organization

1. How is administrative policy formed?

   _____

   _____

2. How are administrative decisions made?

   _____

   _____

3. What are the actual lines of accountability among the pastor, the pastoral council, the youth ministry commission, the youth ministry leadership team, the administrators, and the staff?

   _____

   _____

4. How do administrators spend most of their time?

_____

5. Does a collaborative relationship exist between administrators and parish structures?

_____

6. What opportunities for professional growth are provided for staff?

_____

Program Participants

1. What has been the number of participants in your programs, early adolescence through young adult, in the last ten years? Are there any trends?

_____

_____

2. Is anything being done for outreach and evangelization of young people who are uninvolved or unchurched?

_____

3. How are participants recruited for programs?

_____

Physical Facilities

1. Do teenagers have an area that is theirs, a place where they can "be at home" in the parish? What is the condition of this area?

_____

_____

2. What is the general condition of each of the buildings used for youth ministry?

_____

_____

3. What is the general condition of the equipment and furnishings used for youth ministry?

_____

_____

4. How do you handle transportation for youth ministry?

_____

_____

Youth Ministry Finance

1. How is the youth ministry budget prepared?

_____

2. What is the history of your youth ministry budget in the last six years? Are there any trends?

_____

_____

3. What guidelines do you have from the parish finance council for the next three years?

_____

4. What percentage of the total parish budget is allocated to youth ministry?

_____

5. If you have a school, what percentage of the total parish budget is allocated to the school?

_____

6. What do you project as your youth ministry budget for each of the next three years?

_____

7. How do you fund the youth ministry budget? Is the method adequate?

_____

_____

Community Trends

What community trends do you need to consider in planning for the next three years?

_____

_____

Survey
Youth Ministry—Tell Us What You Think

Our parish youth ministry commission is beginning the process of developing a long-range plan for pastoral ministry among young people. In an effort to gather data that will help make sure we are on target as we plan for the future, we ask you to fill out this form and return it to the planning committee.

Check your age-group:
____ 10- to 14-year-olds
____ 15- to 18-year-olds
____ 19- to 25-year-olds
____ 26- to 40-year-olds
____ 41- to 65-year-olds
____ 66-year-olds and up

1. Look over the following list of issues that young people face and check the five that you think are the most important for us to consider as we plan for youth ministry in our parish. Feel free to add your own issues if they are not on this list.

____ school issues

____ tough family issues

____ alcohol and drug abuse

____ sexual behavior

____ depression and suicide

____ consumerism and materialism

____ salvation issues

____ women's role in the church

____ career and vocational decisions

____ prejudice and racism

____ communication between teenagers and parents

____ stresses and pressures

____ separation and divorce

____ death and dying

____ poverty

others:

____ _____

____ _____

____ _____

Handout 5–D: Permission to reproduce this handout for program use is granted.

2. Rank in order the ten most important needs that you think the young people in our parish have. Use **1** for the most important, **2** for the next most important, and so on. Please add any missing needs to the list. Give specific examples in each need area if any come to mind.

_____ the need for youth ministry to be valued as an important part of the ministries of the parish

_____ the need for more positive adult involvement in parish youth ministry

_____ the need for more young people to have a voice in what goes on in the parish, especially if it involves them

_____ the need for more places where young people can meet and feel at home in our parish

_____ the need for a more effective religious education program

_____ the need for more involvement in parish worship experiences

_____ the need for effective retreat opportunities

_____ the need for physical development and athletic activities

_____ the need for counseling and support group opportunities

_____ the need for more community building and social activities, such as camping trips, lock-ins, dances, and the like

_____ the need for more learning experiences on justice and peace

_____ the need for more service opportunities

_____ the need for more scriptural study and prayer experiences

_____ the need for effective youth leadership training

_____ the need for ethnic and cultural diversity and awareness

_____ the need to learn more about sexuality and life choices

_____ the need for opportunities to develop self-esteem and self-worth

others:

_____ _____

_____ _____

_____ _____

Parish Data Analysis

A. Having looked over the data in the youth ministry assessment and environmental scan report, you probably have some insight into the following four areas. Jot down your thoughts below.

1. What are our youth ministry strengths?

2. What are our youth ministry weaknesses?

3. What new opportunities do you see for our youth ministry?

4. What major concerns do you have about our youth ministry?

B. After reading all the strengths, weaknesses, opportunities, and concerns that people have listed on the newsprint, list your three priorities in each area.

Strengths

1.

2.

3.

Opportunities

1.

2.

3.

Weaknesses

1.

2.

3.

Concerns

1.

2.

3.

C. After sharing your priorities with your group, write down the ten items that your group decided need to be addressed in the future.

1.

2.

3.

4.

5.

6.

7.

8.

9.

10.

Goal Setting

Write down the item that is to be addressed:

_____

_____

_____

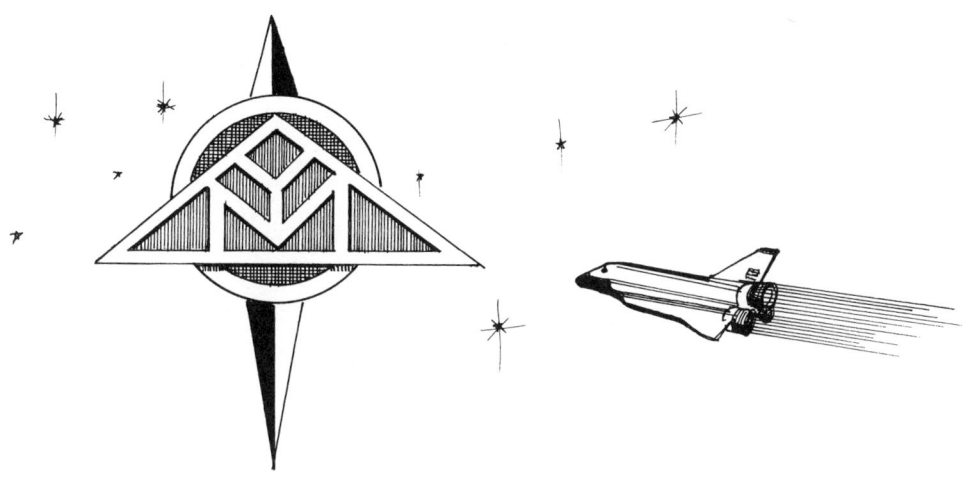

Respond to the following questions. This should give your group the basis for setting a long-range goal.

1. What do we want the present situation to look like in three years? (What should be happening that is not happening? How will we be able to measure the difference? Given our past history, is it realistic?)

3. How committed are we to achieving the goal stated in question 1?

2. How will we know when we have achieved our goal? (What will be the final product or method of measuring success?)

4. How will accomplishing this goal fit in our overall mission? (Review your mission statement to see how well the goal furthers your total mission.)

A List of Verbs for Setting Objectives

Objective-setting should be action oriented. It needs to lead the group to accomplish something. Selecting the right verb to begin a good statement is a step in the right direction.

The following list of possible verbs for objective-setting might be helpful as you begin this process:

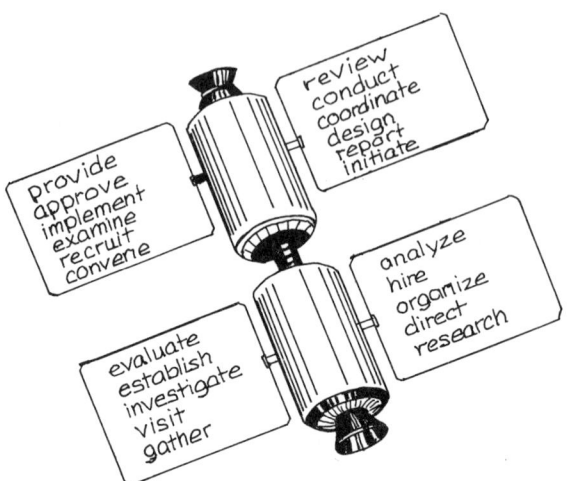

- provide
- visit
- approve
- implement
- hire
- examine
- initiate
- recruit
- evaluate
- establish
- review

- coordinate
- analyze
- design
- report
- organize
- research
- direct
- conduct
- convene
- gather
- investigate

Handout 5–G: Permission to reproduce this handout for program use is granted.

Evaluating Goals and Objectives

Yes ___ No ___   **1.** Is the plan realistic in terms of time?

Yes ___ No ___   **2.** Is the plan realistic in terms of personnel?

Yes ___ No ___   **3.** Is the plan realistic in terms of finances?

Yes ___ No ___   **4.** Will we know when we have achieved our plan?

Yes ___ No ___   **5.** Are we committed to achieving our plan?

Yes ___ No ___   **6.** Does this plan further our pastoral mission?

Handout 5–H: Permission to reproduce this handout for program use is granted.

A Youth Ministry Planning Schedule

July

      1 Leadership Team Meeting
   7–9 Camping Trip
     11 Canoe Trip
     15 Open Gym and Drop-in
     19 Youth Mass and Picnic
24–25 Coed Softball Tournament
     29 Faith Night (Topics listed in newsletter)

August

      1 Junior High Dance
      5 Open Gym and Drop-in
     12 Roller Skating
     14 Swim Party
     19 Open Gym and Drop-in
21–23 Service Plunge
     23 Youth Mass
     26 Bible Sharing

September

      2 Leadership Team Meeting
      6 Back-to-School Mass and Brunch
      9 Open Gym and Drop-in
     16 Faith Night
     23 Open Gym and Drop-in
25–26 Growing Up Sexual
     27 Youth Mass
     27 Road Trip
     30 Faith Night

The remaining months on the calendar would have similar schedules.

Please help us evaluate the youth ministry programs that our parish offered this past year. Place a check in front of each activity that you participated in. Then by circling a letter to the right of each activity, grade how effective it was in meeting your needs. The letters range from A = very effective to F = not effective. Next, put a star to the left of the activity or activities that absolutely should be offered next year. Add any comments you may have about a particular activity.

___ ski trip   A B C D F

___ volleyball league   A B C D F

___ weekly prayer group   A B C D F

___ religious education classes   A B C D F

___ confirmation preparation   A B C D F

___ summer camping trip   A B C D F

___ open gym and drop-in   A B C D F

___ retreat   A B C D F

_____

_____

_____

_____

_____

Are there any other programs or activities that we should consider offering next year? _____

_____

_____

_____

_____

CHAPTER 6

Contracting a Youth Ministry Coordinator

Questions for Reflection

- When you were a teenager, what adult had the most influence on your spiritual growth? What were that person's most important character traits?
- If one person is responsible for coordinating a comprehensive youth ministry program, what skills and traits should that person possess?
- What does the term *ministry* mean to you?

What Is a Youth Ministry Coordinator?

Suppose for a moment that you wanted to find someone to coach a school volleyball team. You would look for an individual with a thorough knowledge of the sport, who is able to work with young people in general. You would also want someone who enjoys working with the team members, helping them improve their athletic performance. Perhaps most important, you would want someone who could help the team make the connection between the sport and life—dealing with challenges, developing positive attitudes, learning new skills, and becoming the best possible volleyball player that each could be.

But now suppose that the person you were seeking was not only to coach the volleyball team but to oversee the whole athletic program—to get coaches for the other sports, to purchase equipment, to schedule games, to oversee the athletic facilities, to connect cheerleading to the sports, to do public relations for the different athletic events—as well as relate it to the mission and goals of the school.

This person would need not only the knowledge and skills of a coach but also administrative skills, management skills, communication skills, interpersonal skills, and the leadership skills to ensure that every athletic event is a well-attended, high-quality event for the team, the school, and the spectators. This person would not merely be a coach, but would be an athletic director.

The difference between a coach and an athletic director is like the difference between a youth minister and a youth ministry coordinator. Hiring a youth minister often means hiring a person to do the work of youth ministry. This work is then usually limited to involving those young people and running those activities that the youth minister has the time and talent for. If she or he does not know much about camping, then the youth of that particular church will probably not experience many camping opportunities. If her or his knowledge of retreat administration is limited, then the young people will probably rarely be offered a parish retreat.

Whereas hiring a youth ministry *coordinator* means hiring a person who not only has the skills and knowledge to work with different aspects of youth ministry but also knows what pieces and arrangements are needed for an entire youth ministry program, and can coordinate them and integrate them with the larger parish ministry.

Many of the parishes I have encountered already have someone working as a youth minister. Many of those youth ministers are capable of being coordinators of youth ministry and are functioning to some extent as coordinators. But the parish primarily expects them to *do* the works of youth ministry rather than *coordinate* those works. It is important to make this distinction.

After years of involvement in youth ministry and after serving on a youth ministry task force for the Archdiocese of Indianapolis, I am convinced that every parish needs a youth ministry coordinator who is responsible for implementing a parish's youth ministry objectives and plans. Depending on the needs and resources of the parish, the coordinator might be a full- or part-time paid employee or a full- or part-time volunteer. In some instances, two or more parishes may hire a coordinator and share that person's time. Regardless of which option is in place, it is imperative that the person assume the role of *coordinator,* that is, to convene, train, and support others who carry out the various events and activities of the parish's youth ministry.

Is the Parish Ready?

When I discussed the establishment of a youth ministry commission in a parish, I talked about the importance of the parish's readiness. The same is true for employing a coordinator of youth ministry. The parish must be ready in three important areas.

Parish support: Leadership groups in the parish (the pastoral council, the board of education, the youth ministry commission, etc.) should be favorable toward promoting youth ministry efforts in the parish. The pastoral staff (the pastor, the director of religious education, the school administrator, etc.) should be in agreement about the need for a coordinator of youth ministry and understand how this role fits with the rest of the staff. There needs to be a broad base of support for the young people of the parish among the parents, adults in general, and parish societies. And finally, there should be a parish policy regarding the reasonable and equitable distribution of resources (financial and other) among all the ministries of the parish.

Financial support: A continual source of frustration for people involved in youth ministry is the attitude of many church members about paying a youth ministry coordinator. "Why should people be paid to work for the church?" they ask. "Why can't people just volunteer? It never cost us anything before." That myth about no cost needs to be dispelled.

In the past the associate pastor's first assignment often included "doing something with the kids." He was the youth minister. No one ever questioned what it cost to have him do this. The cost of youth ministry was hidden within the salary and room and board that he received. But in reality it was costing the parish to have a ministry to young people—youth ministry has never been free. With clergy no longer available to coordinate or do youth ministry, we need to invest money in lay ministers.

Also, decisions regarding the parish's willingness to invest in youth ministry should be based on the skills and knowledge needed, not just on the lowest amount of money it will cost. We need to avoid the trap of the minimalist approach, spending just enough to get by.

Resources: A youth ministry coordinator needs office space along with other appropriate resources, such as a desk, chairs, a phone, file drawers, and a computer or a typewriter. These are no different from the resources needed by any member of the parish pastoral staff, whether it be the pastor, the religious education director, or the parish secretary.

Pre-Search Preparation

The following items should be in place before you conduct a search for a coordinator. If a youth ministry commission already has been established, it will be responsible for this preparation. If not, then an ad hoc committee may need to be set up to accomplish these tasks.

- Form or update the mission statement for youth ministry in the parish.
- Write a job description.
- Decide what requirements, qualifications, and background someone should possess to best fill the position.
- Determine a salary scale based on education, experience, and work expectations. Once you have determined the salary scale, seek approval from the pastoral council in conjunction with the parish finance council.
- Discuss the practical logistics of setting up a youth ministry office, if one is not already in place. For example, decide where the office will be located, what equipment is needed, and so on.

- Write a parish profile. Include parish statistics, history, and other relevant information. Point out areas that make the parish unique and why someone would want to be employed there. See sample 6–A, "A Parish Profile."
- Design or obtain an application form. See sample 6–B, "An Application for Employment."

Specifying Qualifications of a Youth Ministry Coordinator

Whether engaging a part-time volunteer or hiring a paid, full-time, professionally prepared person as coordinator of youth ministry, the parish has a right to expect certain qualifications and characteristics of the person who will be helping in the spiritual development of its young people. In light of heightened public awareness of child sexual abuse by individual youth workers and clergy, parents are very cautious about who is hired to work closely with their children.

The following is a list of possible qualifications for a person who might work as a youth ministry coordinator.

Spiritual Qualifications

On a spiritual level a youth ministry coordinator should be the following:
- a person committed to Jesus Christ and his church and devoted to spreading the Gospel; someone who shows maturity, prayerfulness, optimism, cheerfulness, patience, prudence, and tact
- a person who has a genuine affection for young people, who works well with persons of various ages and backgrounds, and who displays personal healthiness in his or her relationships
- a person who communicates well, in both one-to-one and group settings

Academic Qualifications

On an academic level a coordinator of youth ministry should offer the following:
- a bachelor's degree (or a plan to obtain a degree) in youth ministry or in a related field, such as theological studies, religious education, pastoral ministry, or counseling
- a knowledge of faith formation in young people and of appropriate ways to minister to young people in light of this knowledge
- the desire and ability to continue to update knowledge and skills for youth ministry by pursuing an advanced degree or enrolling in workshops, seminars, conferences, and the like (The parish might offer financial assistance, especially for in-service opportunities.)

Professional Qualifications

On a professional level a coordinator of youth ministry should offer the following:
- several years' experience working with young people (e.g., as a member of a retreat team, in volunteer work with teenagers for a civic or community agency, or at the parish level as a youth ministry volunteer)
- a willingness to understand your community
- the knowledge and skills to carry out these administrative duties:
  - organize and maintain the parish youth ministry office
  - develop policies, goals, and reports
  - involve parish staff, parents, and visitors in youth activities
  - plan a budget and oversee finances
  - act as a liaison between young people and parish organizations
  - work closely with other parish structures that affect youth ministry

Remember that the coordinator of youth ministry must not only coordinate the youth ministry efforts themselves but also coordinate the youth ministry efforts with the rest of the parish's pastoral activities. The coordinator needs to work cooperatively with the pastor, the parish staff, the pastoral council, and any others who are responsible for pastoral ministry in the parish.

Establishing a Just Salary

If your church decides to hire a full- or part-time coordinator of youth ministry or to promote the current youth minister to this position, the first question that will be asked is, How much will it cost? Determining a just salary for a youth ministry coordinator is an important decision. It gives a clear message of the value the parish places on its ministry to young people. It can also help determine the quality, skills, and experience that a parish can expect in the person hired.

If you were to take a poll of the salaries of people in youth ministry across the country, you would find a broad range from low salaries to fairly comfortable ones. On the other hand, the range of job expectations—while just as broad—starts high and rises to nearly impossible levels.

As a church, we need to seriously consider the messages our bishops give us in their pastoral letter on justice and the economy. Employees of the church are entitled to a just salary with reasonable benefits (*Economic Justice for All* [Washington, DC: USCC, 1986], no. 351).

A good place to begin determining a fair salary for a youth ministry coordinator is the local public school system. What are teachers being paid? Contact the school district's office and ask for a copy of teacher salaries based on education and experience. If you are hiring a youth ministry coordinator with a bachelor's degree and five years' experience, that person should be making *at least* as much as a parish or local public schoolteacher with the same qualifications. Also, if the youth ministry coordinator's responsibilities span a full twelve months, take into consideration that schoolteachers' salaries are usually for a nine-month commitment. Additionally, the coordinator's job includes a lot of administrative responsibilities that a teacher's job does not. The coordinator should be compensated for that. Handout 6–A, "Computing a Youth Ministry Coordinator's Salary," offers other helpful considerations and suggestions.

Developing a Job Description

The job description for a coordinator of youth ministry should be based on the needs and goals of youth ministry in the parish. Because those needs and goals change on a regular basis, the job description might have to be altered from year to year. It should be developed and updated by the youth ministry commission.

A simple process for developing a job description for a youth ministry coordinator follows:

- Brainstorm the primary roles and tasks that a youth ministry coordinator would have in your parish. Do this without any discussion or evaluation, just pure brainstorming.
- Once a list of roles and tasks is composed, spend some time discussing and then prioritizing them.
- Categorize the roles and tasks under the seven components of youth ministry outlined in *A Vision of Youth Ministry*. Specify the functions of each item under each component of ministry.

Incorporating the Components of Youth Ministry

Here are the seven components of youth ministry from *A Vision of Youth Ministry* and examples of roles and tasks for the coordinator.

Word: The ministry of the word is the sharing of the Gospel message of the good news of God's love and salvation as lived by Jesus. The coordinator's responsibilities could include the following:

- Be responsible for or be involved in the religious education program and the confirmation program for young people.
- Maintain personal, professional, and spiritual development through course work, reading, seminars, workshops, or retreats.

Worship: The ministry of worship celebrates the relationship between young people and their God. This is expressed through a variety of liturgical and paraliturgical formats. The coordinator's responsibilities could include the following:

- Work with the liturgy committee to involve young people in the parish's worship experiences.
- Facilitate the planning and implementation of special youth worship services.

Creating community: The ministry of creating community is the development of relationships in the lives of young people that enable them to grow in faith—a reaching out to young people, calling them forth to share in the celebration of a Christian community. The coordinator's responsibilities in this area could include the following:

- Be involved with the long-range planning committee of the commission in doing needs assessment, setting goals and objectives, and developing action plans for the parish youth ministry.
- Establish adult-youth teams for overseeing youth activities.
- Encourage adult youth workers to develop one-on-one relationships with some of the young people.

Guidance and healing: The ministry of guidance and healing provides an opportunity for young people to share the needs of their lives, to be listened to, to be reconciled, and to be healed. The coordinator's responsibilities could include the following:

- Be present to young people and, to the extent possible, get to know them personally so that you can listen to and guide them.
- Initiate and oversee training opportunities in guidance and healing ministries for adult and youth volunteer leaders and workers.

Justice and service: The ministry of justice and service gives young people an opportunity to use their gifts of energy, idealism, and enthusiasm to transform the world into a just place, where all people are treated with respect and dignity and are served. The coordinator's responsibilities could include the following:

- Develop a knowledge of the parish's and local community's service organizations and establish a rapport with these organizations.
- Initiate and oversee justice and service awareness workshops, both for youth workers and for the youth community.
- Make sure that service opportunities are part of the youth ministry program.

Enablement: The ministry of enablement is the calling forth and development of the gifts of young people and adults who work with them. This is done in order that they might lead, grow, and minister. The coordinator's responsibilities could include the following:

- Develop and maintain teams of leaders and workers to direct and carry out the youth ministry programs, events, and activities.
- Select and gather appropriate resources for the parish youth ministry.
- Administer the youth ministry budget.

Advocacy: The ministry of advocacy means listening, caring, and interpreting. To be an advocate is to be a voice for those who do not have a voice that is listened to. The coordinator's responsibilities could include the following:

- Maintain communication with the parish at large, the parish staff, the youth ministry leaders and workers, and the administrators, teachers, and staff in the local high schools.
- Participate in pastoral staff meetings and meetings of the parish pastoral council.
- Prepare and submit written reports to the youth ministry commission, to the pastor, and to the pastoral council on a regular basis.
- Advocate for youth needs and activities to the broader community.
- Maintain a liaison with other levels of structures for youth ministry, that is, deanery, diocesan, regional, or national.

Obviously, a part-time volunteer youth ministry coordinator cannot be expected to be as involved as someone who is full-time and paid. A job description for a youth ministry coordinator should be designed relative to the work time and pay that is agreed on.

The Search Process

The process of searching for a coordinator of youth ministry consists of the following steps:

1. Appoint a search committee. The search committee should include representatives from the youth ministry commission, the youth ministry staff, and the adults and young people of the parish. A chairperson should be appointed. I recommend that an adult, perhaps one from the youth commission, fill this role.

2. Begin advertising. Advertise in your parish bulletin and the bulletins of neighboring parishes, your own diocesan newspaper, as well as other diocesan papers. If you are looking to a broader audience, you might include a national Catholic newspaper. Contact your diocesan youth ministry or religious education office and ask to have your job opening put on their list. Oftentimes people contact them about job openings. Send notices to Catholic colleges, seminaries, and universities. Your advertisement might read something like this:

> Full-time youth ministry coordinator needed to coordinate a team approach to holistic youth ministry. Training and experience in the area of youth ministry required. College degree preferred. For application, send a resume to [include here the name of a contact person and the parish's name and address]. Resumes need to be received by [date].

3. Send applications. When someone inquires about the job, send an application to them. Give them a date by which it should be returned.

4. Review the applications. Review the applications and determine the number of applicants that you want to interview. You might begin with your top three choices. Contact those to be interviewed and arrange a time for the interview. Also contact their references. (See sample 6–C, "A Reference Form.")

5. Interview the applicants. If more than three people are on the interview team, one person should be designated to ask the questions; the others should listen. At the end of the interview, the others might ask any clarifying questions. It is important that the applicant not feel overwhelmed by multiple questions from a large search committee.

Two hours is usually sufficient for a good interview. Have your interview questions planned and be prepared to answer questions about the parish and the position. Remember that the applicant is also interviewing you and looking over the parish to determine if she or he wants the job. (See appendix J, "Interview Guidelines.") Normally the parish is expected to pay travel expenses incurred by interviewees.

After the interview, the interview team should immediately spend some time reflecting on the interview and the applicant. (See handout 6–B, "Evaluation of Interviewed Applicant.") During this time other members of the youth ministry team can give the applicant a tour of the parish facilities, the parish neighborhood, or other areas of interest.

6. Respond. Respond to all applicants whether interviewed or not, stating whether they are being considered for the position. Do this as soon as possible. Informing applicants of their status in writing is an important ethical issue. For people not being considered, it is important that they not be left hanging.

7. Recommend. When the interviews are completed, a person or a slate of candidates is recommended to the youth ministry commission and then to the pastoral council and the pastor.

The Hiring Process

Once the pastoral council and the pastor have approved a person or selected from the candidates you have recommended, send a formal letter offering a contract to the individual. The letter should include the salary offer, the job benefits, the starting date of the job, and the duration of the contract. Request a date by which you will need a response. Initially, the offer can be made by phone, but a formal letter should follow to document the offer.

Include the following elements in the contract:
- the name and location of the parish
- the full name of the youth ministry coordinator to be hired
- dates of the term of employment (The recommended term of employment is a minimum of one year and is renewable upon mutual agreement.)
- the salary and schedule of payments
- the job benefits, such as insurance, pension, transportation, allowance for meals, education, vacation, sick leave
- details concerning termination
- signature lines for the pastor, the pastoral council chairperson, and the youth ministry commission chairperson, as well as that of the person to be hired

A copy of the job description should accompany the contract. When both parties agree on the terms of the contract, it is signed by the people listed at the bottom of the contract. (See sample 6–D, "A Contract for a Youth Ministry Coordinator.")

The Commissioning

Once you have contracted for the services of a youth ministry coordinator, whether paid or volunteer, this individual should be commissioned before a parish assembly. Have a reception after the commissioning so that people in the parish can get to know the new coordinator. (See sample 6–E, "A Commissioning Ceremony for a Youth Ministry Coordinator.")

A Parish Profile

Saint Mary's Parish
P.O. Box 100
Youthtown, IN 20202
Phone: 333-456-1234

Pastor: Rev. John Smith
Location: Rural
Parish staff: Pastor, secretary, coordinator of religious education

Membership: Three hundred households, family oriented, large percentage of young people

Characteristics: Moderate income; culturally diverse; active lay participation, sharing parish responsibilities and leadership; active pastoral council and board of education

Community description: Youthtown has a mixed heritage with a strong sense of community and stability. Many of the families' ancestors came here several generations ago, but the community also includes new families. Located in beautiful rolling hill country, it has close proximity to a big city.

Parish plant: A small wood-frame church, a rectory, a parish hall, an activities building with a gym, a religious education center, and a cemetery.

Schools: Most students attend the central public junior and senior high school. Several attend the regional Catholic high school.

We feel that a youth ministry coordinator would enjoy working at Saint Mary's because of the support of the parish and the community and our willingness to share faith with our young people.

An Application for Employment

To properly evaluate your application, it is essential that all the following questions be answered carefully and completely.

Name: _____ Date: _____
       (last)   (first)   (middle initial)

Present address: _____

City: _____ State: _____ Zip: _____

Home phone: _____ Work phone: _____

Soc. sec. no.: _____

When can you start work? _____

Have you been employed previously by a parish or diocese? _____
If yes, please give the following information:

When	Where	Title
_____	_____	_____
_____	_____	_____

What is your present physical condition? _____
_____
_____

Have you ever been convicted of a crime? _____ If yes, please explain:
_____

Educational Background

Name and location	Years	Degree	Major
High school			
_____	_____	_____	_____
Technical school			
_____	_____	_____	_____
College			
_____	_____	_____	_____
Graduate school			
_____	_____	_____	_____

List any other educational experiences related to work with young people:
_____
_____

Military Record

Service branch: _____ Date entered: _____

Final rank: _____ Date discharged: _____

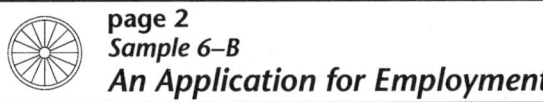
Work Experience

List positions in chronological order, starting with your current or most recent experience. List all jobs held during the last ten years. Add more sheets if necessary.

Employer name: _____

Dates of employment: _____

Address: _____

City: _____ State: _____ Zip: _____

Phone: _____ Supervisor: _____

Area of responsibility: _____

Employer name: _____

Dates of employment: _____

Address: _____

City: _____ State: _____ Zip: _____

Phone: _____ Supervisor: _____

Area of responsibility: _____

Employer name: _____

Dates of employment: _____

Address: _____

City: _____ State: _____ Zip: _____

Phone: _____ Supervisor: _____

Area of responsibility: _____

List any additional experience in youth work not indicated above:

_____

_____

References

List two professional references and two personal references:

Name: _____ Phone: _____

Address: _____

City: _____ State: _____ Zip: _____

Reference is professional _____ personal _____ (check one).

Name: _____ Phone: _____

Address: _____

City: _____ State: _____ Zip: _____

Reference is professional _____ personal _____ (check one).

Name: _____ Phone: _____

Address: _____

City: _____ State: _____ Zip: _____

Reference is professional _____ personal _____ (check one).

Name: _____ Phone: _____

Address: _____

City: _____ State: _____ Zip: _____

Reference is professional _____ personal _____ (check one).

Of the jobs you have held, which did you like most and why?

_____

_____

Of the jobs you have held, which did you like least and why?

_____

_____

May we contact your present employer? Yes No (Circle one.)

List community activities, volunteer work, or professional organizations in which you have participated:

_____

_____

State why you are applying for this youth ministry position:

_____

_____

_____

_____

Read this statement carefully before signing: The facts set forth above are true and complete. I understand that false statements on this application form may be considered sufficient cause for dismissal.

_____   _____
(signature)   (date)

Please return to
Rev. John Smith
Youth Ministry Search Committee
Saint Mary's Parish
P.O. Box 100
Youthtown, IN 20202

Computing a Youth Ministry Coordinator's Salary

Base Salary

Determine the base salary by using the teacher's
starting salary scale for your parish or local public schools. $_____

Other Salary Considerations

Education and Experience

Education

- a bachelor's degree with twelve hours (undergraduate
  or graduate) in youth ministry, theology, or religious
  studies (add 2.5 percent of base salary) $_____

- a single master's degree with an additional twelve
  graduate hours in pastoral theology, religious studies, or
  youth ministry (add 7.5 percent of base salary) $_____

- a second master's degree in theology, youth ministry,
  pastoral ministry, religious studies, or education with a
  focus in theology or religious studies (add 15 percent of
  base salary) $_____

Experience

- number of years of experience in parish administration
  of youth ministry (add 1.25 percent of base salary for
  each year) $_____

Management Responsibilities

Size of Parish

- over 3,000 parishioners (add 5 percent of base salary) $_____

- from 2,000 to 3,000 parishioners (add 4 percent of
  base salary) $_____

- from 1,000 to 1,999 parishioners (add 3 percent of base
  salary) $_____

- from 500 to 999 parishioners (add 2 percent of base
  salary) $_____

- under 500 parishioners (add 1 percent of base salary) $_____

Scope of Responsibility Beyond Older Adolescents
(15- to 18-year-olds)

- early adolescents (10- to 14-year-olds)
  (add 0.5 percent of base salary) $_____

- young adults (19– to 30-year-olds)
  (add 0.5 percent of base salary) $_____

- other, for example, family-centered programming or
  marriage preparation (add 0.5 percent of base salary for
  each) $_____

Number of Personnel Supervised
Personnel who are directly accountable to the coordinator,
including catechists, custodians, secretaries, aids (both
volunteer and paid)

- up to 10 persons (add 10 percent of base salary) $_____
- up to 25 persons (add 15 percent of base salary) $_____
- more than 25 persons (add 20 percent of base salary) $_____

Work Hours
The normal work week should be 40 hours. Additional
hours per week should be compensated.

- average 41 to 50 hours (add 2.5 percent of base salary) $_____

- average 51 or more hours a week (add 5 percent of base
  salary) $_____

Total Salary $_____

Employer's Portion of FICA $_____

Fringe Benefits
(not subject to withholding) $_____
- health and life insurance for coordinator and dependents
- retirement program
- professional in-service allowance
- retreat allowance
- paid vacation time
- sick leave

Total Salary and Benefits $_____

Applicant: _____

Address: _____

City: _____ State: _____ Zip: _____

Reference: _____

Occupation: _____

Address: _____

City: _____ State: _____ Zip: _____

Phone: _____ Best time to call: _____

Thank you for agreeing to provide a reference on behalf of the applicant named above, who is seeking the position of youth ministry coordinator at Saint Mary's Parish in Youthtown, Indiana.

Approximately how long have you known the applicant and in what capacity?

Please describe the applicant's effectiveness in working with young people.

Please describe the applicant's effectiveness in working with adults.

What particular gifts and talents would he or she bring to this position?

Please rate the level of the following qualities and skills of the prospective employee. In the space before each quality or skill, place your rating, using the following scale. Write *NK* if you have no knowledge of an area. Feel free to write additional comments.

1	*2*	*3*	*4*	*5*
•	•	•	•	•
Weak		**Medium**		**Strong**

_____ Ability to relate well with young people
Comments:

_____ Confidence in self
Comments:

_____ Honesty and openness in relationships
Comments:

_____ Development of own faith-life
Comments:

_____ Witness to the Christian faith through his or her lifestyle
Comments:

_____ Openness to spiritual growth
Comments:

_____ Openness to new learning
Comments:

_____ Reliability
Comments:

_____ Ability to express self
Comments:

_____ Ability to take criticism
Comments:

_____ Ability to work with superiors
Comments:

_____ Ability to work as a part of a team
Comments:

Evaluation of Interviewed Applicant

Person interviewed: _____

Interviewer: _____

Date: _____

Ability to Communicate
_____ good
_____ moderate
_____ poor
Comments:

Relating Orientation
_____ relates heavily out of emotions
_____ relates heavily out of intellect
_____ good integration of intellect and emotions in relating
Comments:

Apparent Commitment to the Job
_____ strong
_____ tentative
Comments:

Spiritual Awareness
Does the person seem to have an awareness of God's presence?
Comments:

Personal Appearance
_____ clean and well-groomed
_____ nondescript
_____ sloppy and unclean

Summary Statement (Pick one.)

_____ I feel that this person is entirely capable of making and carrying out a commitment to this job.

_____ I am not sure that this person can make and carry out a commitment to this job, for the following reasons:

_____

_____

_____

_____ I feel that this person is not ready to make and carry out a commitment to this job, because of these reasons:

_____

_____

_____

Sample 6-D
A Contract for a Youth Ministry Coordinator

Employer, name of parish pastoral council:

_____

(Hereinafter referred to as the Pastoral Council)

Name and location of the parish:

_____

Name of the youth ministry coordinator to be hired:

_____

(Hereinafter referred to as the Coordinator)

Term of contract: From the [day] of [month], 19[year], to the [day] of [month], 19[year].

Salary: $_____ per contract year
Salary shall be paid semimonthly in twenty (ten-month contract) _____ or twenty-four (twelve-month contract) _____ equal payments. (Check one.)

Benefits: [List.]

Value of the benefits: $_____
Total value of salary and benefits: $_____

IN ACCORDANCE with the declarations above, the Pastoral Council agrees to hire and the Coordinator agrees to serve for the duration of this contract on the following terms:

1. The Pastoral Council shall pay the Coordinator the salary designated above and provide the benefits listed.

2. If the parish is closed before the end of the duration of this contract, the Coordinator's salary shall not abate, unless this contract is otherwise lawfully terminated.

3. This contract shall not be terminated or withdrawn without cause. The Pastoral Council, with the approval of the Pastor, may terminate or withdraw this contract for any of the following causes on the part of the Coordinator:
- failure to perform the duties of the job
- job-related conduct seriously impairing the credibility of the Coordinator and/or seriously impairing the Coordinator's usefulness in carrying out the duties of the position
- personal conduct or lifestyle at variance with the policies of the diocese or the moral and religious teachings of the Catholic church
- any material falsification in the Coordinator's application for employment, which is made a part of this contract

The coordinator shall not be entitled to salary after such termination or withdrawal of this contract.

4. This contract is not automatically renewable. A new contract may be withheld without cause.

5. This contract supersedes all prior oral or written agreements and can be modified only by a mutual agreement in writing signed by both parties.

IN WITNESS WHEREOF, the parties have hereunto set their hands at _____.
Date: _____

_____ Date: _____
(signature of youth ministry coordinator to be hired)

_____ Date: _____
(signature of youth ministry commission chairperson)

_____ Date: _____
(signature of pastoral council chairperson)

_____ Date: _____
(signature of pastor)

Sample may not comply with local laws.

A Commissioning Ceremony for a Youth Ministry Coordinator

The pastor or pastoral council chairperson calls the person who has been chosen by the parish to serve as the coordinator of youth ministry. The person comes forward carrying a lighted candle and stands facing the assembly.

Opening Words

You have been chosen to coordinate youth ministry at [name of parish] and lead the year. As a member of our parish pastoral staff, you are called to be a faithful follower of Christ and a servant to young people. May your work of coordination and leadership be filled with the light of Jesus. May his love take root in your life, may he strengthen you in times of challenge, and may he guide you with his wisdom in all that you do.

Statement of Intentions

I now ask you to state your intentions before the community assembled here. [After each question, the coordinator responds, "I do."]

- Do you pledge to allow your faith to shine before all through your words and actions? [I do.]
- Do you promise to fulfill to the best of your abilities the duties of your position? [I do.]
- Do you pledge to be a cooperative and supportive member of our parish and to value highly the needs of our young people? [I do.]
- Do you accept this challenge with trust that God's strength will be there to help you fulfill it? [I do.]

Closing Prayer

Creator God, we thank you for having called [name] to serve our parish. Continue to give [name] the courage and faith to carry out this ministry to our young people. Strengthen [name] with your love and peace, Lord. Bless [name] in the name of the Father, and of the Son, and of the Holy Spirit. Amen.

Let us show our approval and affirmation of [name], whose commitment we have witnessed here! [Applause.]

CHAPTER 7

Building a Pool of Volunteers

Questions for Reflection

- Make a list of the characteristics of adults you know who are able to relate well to young people.
- What do you think is the greatest fear that keeps adults from getting involved with young people? Why?
- What steps do you think are important for recruiting and supporting youth workers?
- How do you avoid burnout?

Character Traits of Youth Ministry Volunteers

The best candidates for volunteer youth ministry work are those who have the following personal characteristics:

Christian faith: They have a willingness to live what they believe and be persons of prayer, both personal and sacramental.

Initiative: They possess an enthusiasm for life and an eagerness to venture into new activities.

Balanced judgment and guidance: They have patience and an awareness of the needs of young people and an appreciation of young people's interests, along with a healthy sense of their own personal needs.

Dependability: They are reliable and faithful in the performance of their duties.

A sense of humor: They are able to laugh at themselves, as well as at some of the crazy situations that occur when working with young people. They are able to create a pleasant and congenial atmosphere that conveys the Good News as just that . . . good!

Good ministerial skills: They have effective skills in communication, planning, making referrals, and the like. These skills do not limit the pool of potential volunteers very much. In fact, I bet that if you sat down right now and thought of the young people and the adults in your parish with these skills, the list would be fairly extensive. Try it. You may find that many dozens of people possess the skills needed to be youth ministry volunteers.

Recruiting Volunteer Youth Ministers

The following guidelines for recruiting youth ministry volunteers can help you attain positive results.

Focus on Short-term Opportunities

People often hesitate to volunteer for church work because the church has an image problem about volunteer services. For example, people often expect volunteer youth ministry leaders to commit most of their free time for a *minimum* of three years. This kind of thinking keeps many people from volunteering their time and talents.

I believe the key to recruiting volunteers for youth ministry is in short-term opportunities that enable volunteers to use their gifts and talents. From the group that has positive experiences through short-term commitments, volunteers willing to make longer commitments will step forward.

One of the best examples of creative thinking in recruiting volunteers comes from Saint Lawrence Parish in Aurora, Indiana. The young people of the parish were planning a service project to help some of the poverty-stricken older people of a nearby community. The youth ministry staff believed one particular member of the parish would work wonderfully with the teenagers. But they previously could not seem to get him interested. The service project called for some building repair work. This man was a carpenter, so they decided to call him before the project to ask if he would be willing to teach the young people some carpentry skills. The teenagers would come to his shop, where he could use his tools in the demonstrations. He agreed.

The guy had a great time with the young people. He taught them all sorts of skills—not just for the service project, but skills they could use for the rest of their lives. The young people thought he was great. Although they had previously seen him every Sunday at liturgy, they had no idea that he cared for them. Now they saw him in a whole new light.

And that was not the ending of a happy story. . . . This carpenter continued to stay involved. He was able to do the things he was good at, and share those with the young people. His commitments were short, manageable lengths of time that fit his busy schedule. Everyone in the group benefited.

In an issue of *Sharing News* (October 1988), Tom Zanzig questions the assumption that effective youth ministry requires extensive, long-term contact between an adult leader and a small group of young people. He summarizes his position with three important points:

- Most people, young and old alike, intuitively connect with some people and remain distant from others.
- If this is true, then the more adults that the young person can be exposed to (and vice versa), the greater the chances for spontaneous, trusting relationships to emerge between them.
- Rather than seeking long-term, in-depth contact between one adult and a group of young people, a goal of youth ministry should be to increase the number of contacts between young people and a variety of adults. Then adult leaders can be encouraged to pursue deeper relationships outside the formal program with those young people with whom they hit it off.

Zanzig refers to this approach as *one-minute ministry*. He further contends:

Faith is shared most effectively not within formally structured programs but within the context of satisfying personal relationships that spontaneously emerge between some adults and some young people. Within those relationships, as within all human relationships, brief and often fleeting moments will occur when the opportunity is presented for the adult to influence the faith development of the young person through a kind word, an attentive ear, or a hug when it is needed. These unstructured and unexpected moments of grace and giftedness are at the very heart of our ministry.

In these times of busy schedules and busy people, youth ministry needs to change its focus from long-term programs with long-term commitments that offer opportunities for only a few leaders, to programming that offers many opportunities to many people for various periods of time. Long programs are not sacred. What is sacred are the caring relationships between adults and young people that can happen within the programs.

Include All Possible Candidates

In the past the church has sought out only adults as prime candidates for doing youth ministry. But more recent experiences in youth ministry have shown that young people have a great capacity to minister to their peers. As I mentioned previously, some of the most effective leader teams are combinations of young persons and adults rather than teams of one or the other. Consequently, both adults and young people themselves should be considered for taking on the tasks of leading, organizing, or assisting with youth ministry events and activities.

Provide Job Descriptions

For every area in which you want to recruit a volunteer leader, a specific job description needs to be developed. The clearer you are about what needs to be done, the better are your chances of recruiting someone to do it. People do not like to guess. I believe the reason a lot of people say no when asked to be involved is that they do not really know what they would be volunteering for.

Specifics to be included in each job description are the following:

- the title of the role (e.g., ski trip coordinator or basketball coach)
- a list of the specific tasks and responsibilities involved
- the skills needed to get the job done
- the length of the commitment
- any specific training needed for the position, and how and when that training can be acquired
- who the volunteer is accountable to and who provides support
- the personal and spiritual benefits that can be expected from the experience

Putting together a good job description is already half the work of recruitment. You have named the task, and you have identified the skills needed to get the job done. Now the critical part is to match the task to a person who has the skills and gifts to accomplish it. Who in the parish or community can accomplish what needs to be done? That is a different question from, Who might be willing to do it if we beg them long enough?

Match Ministry Needs with People's Talents

Matching the ministry needs with people's talents can be done in several ways. A parishwide time and talent survey would be a big help, especially if this has been compiled on a computer. If information is not available in this fashion, what are your other sources of information? Does the parish staff know anyone? Ask the young people who they know of that would be good. Often they come up with a great list of names. If you have a youth ministry commission, it can be an excellent resource. Also, as you begin to recruit volunteers, they in turn may know of others who are both qualified and willing.

Make Personal Contact

Once you have identified someone who you believe would get the job done, the next step is to contact them. The best way is by personal contact, especially by someone the potential volunteer knows. The coordinator of youth ministry in a parish is usually a good person to make the contact. But youth ministry commission members could do it. And in some cases, let the young

people ask. It makes quite an impact on adults when they realize that young people look up to and respect them, and believe they would do an excellent job in a specific area of youth ministry.

One of the most effective approaches that I have seen for making contact with potential volunteers and matching jobs with interests and skills took place in a small rural parish in southern Indiana. Those responsible for youth ministry had invited the parish to come to a meeting to learn more about youth ministry. Adults and young people were both welcome. The young couple in charge had done a good job of talking up the event and advertising it so that people were curious. Job descriptions had been prepared for all the tasks for the entire year. These job descriptions were taped to the wall, amidst an attractive display of pictures and diagrams depicting previous ministry. The job descriptions clearly stated the length of a job commitment, most of which were short-term.

Before the meeting was over, people were scrambling to take the various job descriptions off the wall to make sure they got to do the jobs. It was a simple process of connecting people who cared about teenagers with short-term tasks that they were comfortable with and would enjoy doing.

Provide Training

Many people have a genuine care and concern for young people and would like to get involved, but do not feel capable. If ways are offered to help them feel competent, then the chance of getting volunteers greatly increases.

Consider offering different training programs for the different types of volunteer work. Sometimes small, short-term tasks require small, short-term training; while larger, longer-term tasks require larger, longer-term training. Be creative, use your imagination, and develop training opportunities that are tailor-made to fit the different types of jobs and the young people and adults who volunteer to lead them.

Chapter 4 offers training and growth suggestions for youth ministry commission members that can also be used for volunteer youth workers.

Supporting and Maintaining a Pool of Volunteers

Studies show that volunteers in nonprofit organizations, especially churches, are the least appreciated and most overworked people around. When people say yes to becoming youth ministers, they need to know that they are going to be supported and affirmed along the way. The following strategies are some proven ways to support and affirm volunteers.

Authorize and Recognize

Being publicly authorized and recognized is a great source of support and affirmation. This can start at the beginning of a volunteer's service through the signing of a contractual agreement, along with a commissioning at a parish liturgy or other gathering. (See sample 7–A, "A Commissioning Ceremony for Youth Ministry Staff and Volunteers.")

Ongoing affirmation and recognition of volunteers can be accomplished in many different ways: dinners, parties, liturgies, gifts, recognition plaques or certificates, and the like. Pay special attention to your volunteers at certain landmarks of service, such as the completion of a significant event or program or a substantial period of involvement. Send them birthday or anniversary cards. Remember them at holidays. You can learn a lot from the business world about how to treat and support volunteers.

Volunteer leaders in youth ministry need recognition not only from those who recruited them but also from the young people they serve and the parish at large. For example, give a recognition dinner for volunteers that is open to the entire parish and that the young people serve; or put a thank-you message in the parish bulletin from the pastoral council.

Establish Support Groups

A large amount of personal energy is invested in volunteering to work with young people, often with little return from the young people in whom the investment is made. Moreover, the business of the work makes it easy for personal reflection and prayer to fall by the wayside. A peer support group can be an answer to this dilemma. Support groups, by sharing the pain and joy, the anxiety and hope, can renew energy that a person cannot renew alone.

Although personal support can come in many contexts—a dinner, a quiet moment with a friend, a lively discussion over a beer—it is most effective when it is intentional, planned, and regular.

Support groups can exist on a number of levels. They might focus on developing skills, providing recreation, praying, sharing resources, or studying together. But their common basis is that God's power and presence are experienced in human exchange, and their overriding purpose is always personal support for one another in carrying out the ministry.

The following are some suggestions for establishing a support group:

- Contact a group of people (four to eight) who might have a common interest in gaining support and who would be comfortable with the personal sharing that is involved in a support group.
- Decide what level of activity would provide the most effective focus for the group.
- Set dates, times, and places for the meetings.
- Determine how responsibilities for meals, costs, facilitating, and so on, are to be shared.
- Make a group covenant to be there for one another.
- Take time for evaluation after each meeting to see how the group is doing.

Establish Boundaries for Healthy Relationships

In light of heightened public awareness of and attention to child protection issues, volunteers need to be alerted to boundaries that assure a safe and healthy relationship between themselves and the young people they work with.

In fact, some parishes or dioceses have specific guidelines established for adult volunteers who work with young people. You may want to check with your diocesan office or your pastor.

Here are some characteristics of an unhealthy or inappropriate relationship:

- The adult depends on being liked by the young person.
- The adult depends on the close, personal friendship of the young person.
- The adult depends on the young person's help in times of difficulty or personal crisis.
- The adult "unloads all" on the young person.
- The adult projects her or his own expectations on the young person.
- The adult engages in any inappropriate sexual behavior consisting of sexual advances, requests for sexual favors, sexually motivated physical conduct, or other verbal or physical conduct of a sexual nature. This may include the following:
  1. subtle or explicit pressure (verbal or physical) for sexual activity
  2. pinching, caressing, fondling, intentional brushing against another's body, inappropriate patting, or any other sexually motivated touching

Provide for Accountability and Evaluation

Providing simple, nonthreatening ways to evaluate the work of volunteers is a great way to give feedback and affirmation. Ask questions like these: What did you enjoy the most? What areas did you see a need to improve on? What would you do differently? Look for ways to affirm the volunteers while they are being critiqued. Tell them what was most helpful in what they did. How did the young people benefit because of their involvement? Help them see the good that they did.

Hold Meaningful Meetings

One of the quickest ways to disillusion youth ministry volunteers is to subject them to meetings that drag on forever and seemingly have no purpose. This may seem like a problem that is simple to correct, but poorly run meetings still plague many parishes—not to mention other organizations and businesses.

Steps can be taken to facilitate an effective meeting. Many of these things are a matter of common sense, and if you have been leading meetings, you probably have been doing them all along. But to see them in writing will make you more conscious of them. And for those of you who will be facilitating meetings for the first time, these hints will be especially timely and helpful.

Setting meeting agendas: Meetings go much smoother if each member of the group has an agenda. Consider doing the following:

- Send the agenda along with the notice about the upcoming meeting. If sending the agenda ahead of time is not possible, it should be distributed at the beginning of the meeting, and the participants should be given time to look it over.
- Insofar as it is possible, provide the participants an opportunity to give input on the formation of the agenda.

Setting up the meeting room: How the meeting room is set up and prepared can make a big difference in how effective the meeting will be. Consider the following ideas:

- Arrange the tables and chairs so that all the participants can see one another. Sitting in a circle or semicircle is helpful especially if you want collaborative input and sharing. Also, sitting alongside one another subtly encourages group bonding.
- Have refreshments available that are appropriate to the age-group. The presence of refreshments creates an atmosphere of hospitality and welcoming.
- Make sure that lighting and ventilation are adequate. The lighting should be appropriate for the kind of meeting you are going to have—for example, dim lighting for a prayer meeting, bright lights for a regular business meeting. Also, the temperature and the ventilation should be such that participants will be comfortable.
- Make name tags or name cards for the participants whenever the people present do not know one another.
- Have extra copies of the agenda (or any background materials) for those who might leave their agenda at home. Bring extra writing materials for those who do not bring any.

Starting the meeting on time: The tone of the meeting is set by what happens in the first few minutes. Consider the following hints:

- Project warmth and enthusiasm for being there. Have a positive attitude. Greet members as they arrive and help them feel welcome.
- Start the meeting on time. If you do not, you discount the members who arrived on time. Starting late will set a precedent that people can come late and still not miss anything.

Conducting the meeting in an orderly manner: An orderly meeting that attends to all the participants is most apt to be a successful meeting. Consider these hints:

- Follow the agenda that was printed and distributed before the meeting.
- Invite equal participation. Be aware if someone or a particular group is dominating the meeting.
- Thank or affirm people who contribute to the purposes of the meeting.
- Listen carefully and establish eye contact with those who are speaking.
- Nurture discussion with appropriate comments.
- Clarify by asking questions, especially if you or other members of the group do not seem to understand.
- Always speak clearly and distinctly so that everyone in the group can hear you without having to strain. Use a microphone if it will help you.
- When a participant is talking, direct the group's attention to him or her.
- Keep the participants directed to the agenda topic at hand. If necessary, limit the time on certain agenda items, especially those items calling for discussion.

Ending the meeting: The way meetings are ended is as crucial to their success as the way they are started. Consider the following strategies:

- Always end on time! An ending time should be agreed on before the meeting and should be adhered to unless the entire group agrees to extend the meeting time.
- Summarize the following for the group:
  - all the decisions that were made at the meeting
  - any assignments that were made (make sure you state *who* is doing *what* and *when*)
  - any communication that is to take place to outside groups or persons
- Remind the participants of the date, time, and place of the next meeting, as well as its agenda highlights. You might even want to gather future agenda items.
- Evaluate the meeting. Participants should have the opportunity to express how they felt about the meeting process.

- End on a positive note. Invite the participants to linger for refreshments and fellowship, especially if there have been significant tensions during the meeting.
- After the meeting, telephone or jot a note to those who were absent and let them know that they were missed. Fill them in on what happened at the meeting.

Dealing with problems at meetings: Even the best facilitator encounters problems at meetings. Being aware of potential problems is the first step in dealing with them. The following are potential problems and suggestions on how to handle them:

The meeting is dragging. Possible solution: Cut out any dead time between agenda items. Facilitate the agenda so that it moves more quickly. Is too much time being spent on issues that may not need it? Check whether any individuals are dominating the meeting.

As chairperson you are doing most of the talking. Possible solution: Cut down on your talking. In the role of the chairperson, it is easy to comment on each issue. Do not do it! People will get the feeling that everything they say is being critiqued and that their input is not valuable.

One or two members are talking most of the time. Possible solution: Invite other members who are quiet to give their input. Consider asking for input with each person getting a turn.

There is not enough time to complete the agenda. Possible solution: Negotiate with the group on how much time to spend on each agenda item and stick to that. Check to make sure that the group is not over-investing time in one area and shortchanging others.

Meetings continually run late. Possible solution: Have the group agree on what time the meeting will end. When that time comes, end it—even if you are not finished. Once this happens one or two times, the group will realize that it needs to move along to get an agenda completed.

A participant is disruptive. Possible solution: Develop a set of norms beforehand that will define appropriate behavior. If this does not work, during a break or after the meeting, confront the individual one-on-one. Use "I feel" statements, not "blaming" language. An "I feel" message uses the following formula: "I feel [feeling] when you [message] because [reason]."

Questions interrupt the flow of the meeting. Possible solution: During a break or after the meeting, state to the questioners that it seems they have a lot of unanswered questions. Ask if you could get that information to them apart from the meeting, so that not as much time is spent on the questions at the meeting.

Some participants are silent. Possible solution: While respecting their choice not to offer input, make sure they feel included. Occasionally direct a question to them if you think they can answer it. Or use a statement like, "You seem to have some ideas regarding the issue. What do you think?"

Individual participants disagree. Disagreement is not necessarily a problem—it can be constructive. But teach the participants to use "I feel" statements when they disagree with one another.

You too might have a whole list of ideas on facilitating effective meetings. Use these, add to them, and develop your personal list.

Provide Adequate Insurance

Make sure that your volunteers and the programs that they are involved in are adequately insured against liability.
- Check whether a youth activity off church grounds is presently covered under the church policy. If not, many insurance companies offer special packages for such events.
- Be aware of the insurance liabilities and the insurance expectations of the facilities you might be using. It is customarily specified in the contract.
- If you rent transportation, check for adequate insurance by the transporting vehicles. Bus rental companies sometimes provide only the bare minimum of liability insurance and expect the renter to be the primary carrier.

Offer Information and Resources

If you are the coordinator, continually look for information and resources that might make the job easier for your volunteers. Helps that facilitate and improve volunteers' work are great morale boosters. Sometimes volunteers just need someone to offer pointers in an affirming manner. The following are areas of information and bits of resources that can easily be overlooked, but which can greatly help volunteers in their work, especially those in leadership roles:

Dealing with policies and rules: Volunteers are often in the position of carrying out rules—rules that should be backed up by policies. Consequently, it is important for them to know the difference between policies and rules.

A policy is a broad guide set by the governing board or commission for discretionary action by the administrator, in this case, the volunteer youth worker. A policy is narrow enough to give clear guidance yet broad enough to permit administrators to use discretion in making decisions and setting rules. For example, if the issue is the extent of parental involvement in youth sacramental preparation, the policy would be the following: *Parents shall be systematically involved in the preparation of their children for the sacraments of reconciliation, Holy Eucharist, and confirmation.*

A rule, on the other hand, is an administrative regulation that specifies a required action. Rule making is a function of the administrator. For example, a rule for carrying out the above policy would be the following: *Parents of children receiving confirmation are required to attend two discussion sessions designed to aid them in preparing their son or daughter for the sacrament. At least one parent needs to attend the sessions.*

A policy is the "what" of the situation and is the concern of the board or commission. The rule is the "who, when, where, and how" and is the function of the administrator.

Some guidelines for recognizing policies and rules are the following:

- If you are talking about next year and years to come, you are making *policy*. If you are talking about next week or next month, you are talking *rules*.
- Policy is a *general* statement of intention. Rules specify how to carry out the intention.

Most seasoned veterans say that it is helpful to have official policy directing the primary areas of an effort in which there are several levels of authority, and that it is crucial that all involved know the difference between policies and rules. I recommend that policy authorization be the role of the pastoral council. The youth ministry commission forms policy for youth ministry, recommends it to the council for authorization, and passes it along to the youth ministry personnel for rule making and implementation.

Identifying and clarifying purposes for gathering young people: Youth ministry in a parish usually includes a variety of youth gatherings. Occasionally the ones who are gathered have a different purpose than the ones who called the gathering. Everyone in a gathering should have the same purpose for being there. If everyone is operating out of the same set of assumptions and expectations, things will go much more smoothly. The following is a list of possible purposes for gatherings in parish youth ministry, with some comments on each:

Building community: Gatherings for building community often have a social character, and young people usually come to them to have fun. And fun is fine. But when you gather young people to build community, do offer opportunities for community to build, opportunities to meet new people and to get to know one another better and on more personal levels. The sky is the limit on the variety of ways that this can be accomplished.

Planning: If you are gathering people to plan, you need to be clear about what you are going to do and who you want to be there. Blanket invitations for this type of gathering lead to trouble. The purpose of planning needs to be clear to the people; otherwise you will have those who simply want to play and who will continually disrupt the planning session.

Disbursing information: This is a common reason for meeting. You gather young people together so you can give them information about upcoming programs, details they need to know, opportunities to sign up for activities or events, and so on. This reason for a gathering usually is not a great drawing card. Disbursing information often needs to be combined with other purposes, such as community building in the form of a pizza party or an ice-cream sundae party. Get the information to them quickly and concisely, and then have fun.

Evaluating: Another good reason to gather young people is to evaluate programs or events. Again, you need to be clear with the young people about what you have planned. This purpose also is not a big drawing card and might be better served if coupled with some fun activity that will bring them in.

Sharing faith and prayer: Gathering young people together for faith sharing and prayer can be a powerful experience for them. It is more important than ever that the purpose be clear to them, so they do not feel like they were tricked into doing something they were not prepared for.

Dealing with a problem: On occasion (I hope you will never have to use this one), it is necessary to gather young people together to deal with a problem. This could be a problem caused by the youth group, like vandalism or cliques, or it might be a problem caused by a happening apart from the group but affecting those in the group, such as a young person getting killed or a fight at a local football game. Gathering young people together to deal with critical issues in their life is an important part of a parish's youth ministry, but be clear about it when you need to do it.

Always remember, the best surprise is no surprise at all. Be clear about the reasons for gathering. If you have people at a gathering who are not there for the intended purpose, accomplishing it may be very difficult.

Assembling a first aid kit: A first aid kit is essential for youth ministers. It will be used for minor scratches, headaches, and sore throats or to provide initial treatment in cases where further medical attention is needed. (See handout 7–A, "First Aid Supplies.")

Keep the contents of the first aid kit dry. Label it well and keep it in plain sight and easy reach in case of an emergency. Always appoint someone on a youth ministry team to be in charge of stocking and dispensing first aid items. Know if there is a doctor, nurse, or any person qualified in first aid on any youth ministry team.

Check for allergies to medicines before giving any. Contact the nearest poison control center for an information packet about poisoning, including poisonous snakebites. Contact your local Red Cross office for a first aid manual.

Use good judgment and caution with medicines. Dispensing or prescribing medications without a license can make one liable. If parents have given permission, it is appropriate to have nonprescription medications available for young people to use at their request. Be sure to check parish or school policy about this.

Using permission slips and medical releases: Permission slips can cause last minute delays, headaches, and an occasional heartbreak for the teenager attempting to board the bus without one. But in the event of an emergency, they can be vitally important. On several occasions, I have been able to secure immediate and necessary medical attention for a young person because of the medical release form. It is sometimes tempting to make an exception and let a person get by without one. Allow no exceptions. The young people will quickly come to know that if they wish to attend church-sponsored events at which the parish might be held liable for injury, accident, or negligence, a permission slip is required. Once the expectation is well understood, you will be surprised how few will forget to comply. Permission slips should grant the following:
- permission to attend a particular event for the dates listed
- permission to secure necessary medical attention
- release of liability in case of injury or accident
  See sample 7–B, "A Permission and Medical Care Release Form." Use it or design one that best meets your needs.

Driving young people to events: In twenty years of work with young people, I have learned a lot about what to do and what not to do when driving young people to youth activities. Many experiences were tough lessons, learned through trial and error. The following is a list of suggestions that can make your life a lot easier if you are responsible for getting and supervising drivers for youth activities, especially activities that require long trips.

Make sure that all the drivers understand and agree with a specific set of rules that they have in hand. A list of suggested rules follows:
- Always obey the speed limit and other traffic laws.
- Stay in an assigned order; do not pass each other or change positions.
- Do not pull up beside other cars to communicate with the people in them unless there is an emergency.
- Always stay in sight of the other cars.
- In the event that you lose a car, the whole group should pull over and let the lost car locate you. Do not have the group split up and try to locate the lost car. Let the drivers know that if they get lost they are to look for the others.
- Each car should have a clear map of the route and destination.
- In the event of a breakdown or problem, one car should go for assistance while all the other cars remain with the one needing repair.
- Always carry a first aid kit and other emergency equipment with you.
- Have extra oil, transmission fluid, and a plastic jug with water along for overheated radiators. (Use great care with hot cars to avoid burns.)
- Never leave on a trip without a usable spare tire that has been checked just before leaving.
- Instruct the drivers that if an exit is missed they should go to the next one and turn around. Never back up on an expressway.
- Make sure all the vehicles are insured adequately. Check the insurance coverage on liability for the owner and for the drivers.
- If possible, all drivers should be adults.
- On a trip, have everyone stop at the same place to eat or use the restroom. You are sure to lose members of the group if you split up and go to several different places.
- Instruct the drivers that in the event of an accident, proper procedures are to be followed, such as having first aid carried out by those who are qualified, notifying police and emergency personnel, looking out for the safety of those in the car, and above all, trying to keep everyone as calm as possible.
- Finally, when a trip involves leaving town, provide the parish or school office with a complete list of those going and the expected time of return, along with your destination and your intended route.

Sample 7–A
A Commissioning Ceremony
for Youth Ministry Staff and Volunteers

On an appropriate day each year, all those who will serve in the parish's youth ministry that year should be commissioned before the parish assembly.

The pastor or the pastoral council chairperson calls forward by name those who will serve in the parish's ministry to young people. They come forward carrying lighted candles and line up facing the assembly.

Opening Words
You have been chosen to serve in the youth ministry efforts of [name of parish] for this coming year. Being a worker in this important ministry to our young people calls you to be a faithful follower of Christ and a servant to young people. May the work that you today are commissioned to do be filled with the light of Jesus. May his love take root in your lives, may he strengthen you in times of challenge, and may he guide you with his wisdom in all that you do.

Statement of Intentions
I now ask you to state your intentions before the community assembled here. [After each question, the group responds, "I do."]
- Do you pledge to allow your faith to shine before all through your words and actions? [I do.]
- Do you promise to fulfill to the best of your ability the duties of your position? [I do.]
- Do you accept this challenge with trust that God's strength will be there to help you fulfill it? [I do.]

Closing Prayer
Creator God, we thank you for having called each of these people to be your servants in the church. Continue to give them the courage and faith to carry out this ministry to our young people. Strengthen them with your love and peace, Lord. Bless them in the name of the Father, and of the Son, and of the Holy Spirit. Amen.

Let us show our approval and affirmation of these people, whose commitment to our youth ministry we have witnessed here! [Applause.]

First Aid Supplies

____ a roll of 1-inch paper tape (hypoallergenic)
____ a roll of sterile gauze
____ adhesive bandages (assorted sizes)
____ two 3-inch-wide elastic bandages
____ five to ten 2-by-2-inch sterile pads
____ ten 4-by-4-inch sterile pads
____ oval gauze eye pads
____ two slings
____ something to use as a tourniquet in case of arterial bleeding
____ splint material
____ one or two instant cold packs
____ small, resealable plastic bags to use for cold packs if ice is available
____ cotton balls
____ a box of matches
____ a tweezers
____ an oral thermometer
____ safety pins (assorted sizes)
____ needles (for removing splinters)
____ a small scissors
____ alcohol wipes or a small bottle of alcohol (for cleaning the thermometer and needles)

____ Betadine wipes (for cleaning cuts)
____ a small bottle of hydrogen peroxide
____ antiseptic ointment
____ calamine lotion
____ analgesic (pain-relieving) lotion (for sunburn)
____ sunscreen
____ a small tube of petroleum jelly (for scratches or chapped lips—never for burns)
____ mentholated cough drops
____ antacid tablets or liquid
____ aspirin
____ aspirin substitute
____ a 1-ounce bottle of syrup of ipecac (to induce vomiting in case of poisoning)
____ a snakebite kit
____ antidiarrhea medicine
____ a decongestant
____ eye drops
____ ammonia ampules (in case of fainting)

Sample 7–B
A Permission and Medical Care Release Form

Participant's name: _____

Date of birth: _____

Father's name: _____ Phone: _____

Address: _____

Place of business: _____ Phone: _____

Mother's name: _____ Phone: _____

Address: _____

Place of business: _____ Phone: _____

Guardian's name: _____ Phone: _____

Address: _____

Place of business: _____ Phone: _____

A local relative or contact person if parents or guardian cannot be reached:

Name: _____ Phone: _____

Address: _____

Relationship: _____

Special considerations to be aware of (allergies, asthma, and so on):

_____

_____

Medications to be taken (list with directions): _____

_____

My child may be given, as necessary:
aspirin yes _____ no _____
aspirin substitute yes _____ no _____

My child _____ has permission to attend _____
and will be responsible for his/her (circle one) own equipment. We will be
leaving at _____ a.m./p.m. (circle one) on _____ (date) and will
return at approximately _____ a.m./p.m. (circle one) on _____
(date). I understand that the cost will be _____ and will make sure my
child does not attend if not feeling well. In case of sickness or accident, the
adults in charge have my permission to secure medical care for my child.

    I release the parish as a corporation, along with persons acting on
behalf of the parish and in accord with parish guidelines for responsible
supervision, from any claims, loss, damage, or expense due to any occur-
rence that injures any person or property during this outing.

_____ _____
    (signature of parent or guardian)   (date)

Sample may not comply with local laws.

Appendices

Principles for Adolescent Catechesis

Foundational Principles

- Adolescent catechesis is situated within the lifelong developmental process of faith growth and of ongoing catechesis. The entire catechetical effort is committed to the continuing faith growth of the individual.
- Adolescent catechesis fosters Catholic Christian faith in three dimensions: trusting, believing, and doing.
- Adolescent catechesis supports and encourages the role of the family and in particular the role of the parent in the faith growth of the young person and involves the parent in formulation of an adolescent catechesis curriculum and in programs to strengthen his or her parenting role.
- Adolescent catechesis respects the unique cultural heritages of young people and builds upon the positive values found in these cultural heritages, while at the same time engaging young people in examining their culture in the light of faith and examining their faith in the light of culture.
- Adolescent catechesis is integrated and developed within a comprehensive, multifaceted approach to ministry with youth.

Operational Principles

- Adolescent catechesis responds to the developmental, social, and cultural needs of adolescence. Related to that, the curriculum respects the changing developmental and social characteristics of the various stages of adolescence, providing a significantly different content and approach for younger and older adolescents.
- Adolescent catechesis respects the variability in maturation rates and learning needs of adolescence.
- Adolescent catechesis respects the expanding freedom and autonomy of adolescents.
- Adolescent catechesis uses a variety of learning formats, environments, schedules, and educational techniques.
- Adolescent catechesis best responds to the learning needs of adolescents when it is focused on particular faith themes.

(Adapted from NFCYM, *The Challenge of Adolescent Catechesis,* pp. 9–10)

Faith Themes for Adolescent Catechesis

In providing a framework for adolescent catechesis, especially in the context of faith themes based on learning needs of older and younger adolescents, six integral dimensions are woven through each of the themes:

- Jesus, his life, and his message are connected in a way that invites young people to a personal response in faith.
- Each faith theme is grounded in the Scriptures.
- The church is a historical community of people committed to the vision, values, and mission of Jesus.
- Adolescents learn to pray by experiencing personal and communal prayer.

- Young people are empowered to live a more faithful, Christian life by action and reflection.
- Young people are enabled to interpret their own culture, society, and life experience in light of the Catholic Christian tradition through critical reflection and interpretation.

Faith Themes for Younger Adolescents

Faith themes were developed for younger adolescents out of the developmental and social readiness of the young people.

Church: Develops an understanding and experience of the Catholic Christian story and mission in order that young people might become involved in the Christian community

Jesus and the Gospels: Allows for the development of a more personal relationship with Jesus that opens young people to knowing, loving, and following him more fully

Morality and decision-making: Enables persons who are becoming increasingly capable of using decision-making skills, and helps them apply Catholic Christian moral values to their life

Personal growth: Enables younger adolescents to develop a stronger and more realistic concept of self by exploring who they are and who they can become

Relationships: Enables younger adolescents to develop more mutual, trusting, and loyal relationships with peers, parents, and other adults by emphasizing skills that enhance and maintain relationships

Service: Explores Jesus' call to live a life of loving service

Sexuality: Helps younger adolescents learn about sexual development while gaining a better understanding of the dynamics of maturing as a sexual person within the values of a mature Catholic Christian

Faith Themes for Older Adolescents

Faith and identity: Develops an appreciation of what it means to be a Christian, a Catholic, and a person of faith

The Gospels: Develops an appreciation of the historical and literary development, structure, and major themes of the four Gospels

The Hebrew Scriptures: Develops an appreciation for the historical and literary development, structure, and major faith themes of the Hebrew Scriptures

Jesus: Develops the meaning of who Jesus is in the context of the older adolescents' lives, what meaning he has for their lives, and how a deep, personal relationship can be experienced with him

Justice and peace: Develops a global social consciousness and compassion that is grounded in the Christian vision and attentive to the needs of those who are hurting or oppressed

Love and lifestyles: Explores the mature sexual identity of the older adolescent, and helps to develop intimate, trusting, and enduring relationships that are lived out through a variety of lifestyles

Morality: Helps internalize a moral value system that enables older adolescents to critique their personal and social values while understanding the role of Christian conscience formation and moral decision-making

Paul and his letters: Develops an understanding of the historical context, literary style, and major themes of Paul's letters, using the insights of scholarship to interpret Paul's writings as an Apostle, preacher, theologian, and man of faith

Prayer and worship: Helps older adolescents develop a personally held spirituality and a rich personal and communal prayer life

(Adapted from NFCYM, *The Challenge of Adolescent Catechesis,* pp. 12–15)

APPENDIX C

Connecting Parents with Their Children

The following suggestions are ways that youth ministry can connect parents with their young people.

Support Family Interaction
- Enable parents as the primary providers of their children's faith formation with suggestions for prayers, seasonal activities, stories, media resources, and other ways to pass on their faith.
- Encourage families to talk about why faith is important and about faith traditions that have been valued within the family for generations.

- Help parents make the most of the limited amount of time they have to spend with their children.
- Help parents understand that school and parish religious education programs are only supplements to what they do to enable their children to grow in faith. Explain how, together, they and the church programs can build a good solid foundation of faith.
- Suggest ways and opportunities for families to celebrate together the value of just being family.

Help Parents Understand Their Adolescents

- Help prepare parents for the onset of puberty in their children so they will know how to deal with the changes that will happen in early adolescence.
- Help parents understand youth culture, how it will influence their children, and how they as parents can talk about it with their children.
- Help parents feel comfortable with their own sexuality and with sharing their values about sexuality with their children.
- Help parents understand why young people act the way they do. Point out that they need to ask, What are the messages young people give us in the way they behave, rather than just the things they say?
- Make available to parents resources (informational as well as counseling) that can assist them in times of crisis. Help them establish support groups so they can share values, frustrations, and stories, or just support one another.

Design Joint Programs for Parents and Adolescents

- Design and offer programs that bring parents and their adolescents together and initiate dialog between them. For example:
  - Offer a course on sexuality for adolescents (which should involve parents anyway). It might include an opening session in which parents are given an overview of what will be taught, followed up with joint discussion with the young people and the adults.
  - Hold a joint session on parent-teen communication.
  - Organize a parent-teen retreat, dance, or intergenerational service project.
  - Lead a joint course based on the developmental needs of parents and teens.
- Design and offer programs that have parallel tracks. For example:
  - If a series is offered for adults on stories from the Hebrew Scriptures, a similar course could be offered at the same time for teenagers. Support or crisis groups can also follow this format (e.g., have the children or the adult children of alcoholics meet while the parent-alcoholics are meeting).

APPENDIX D

Developing a Family Perspective in Youth Ministry

The following suggestions can help church leaders plan for youth ministry with a family perspective.

- Keep up-to-date with family changes and trends.
- Be sensitive to the many kinds of families participating in your programs, not only to the "traditional" family.
- Be sensitive to the special needs families experience and to the pressures and stresses these needs create for the family.
- Help families realize that it is socially acceptable and responsible to turn to others for help when they experience special needs.
- Be sensitive to the time and energy commitments of families in which both parents—or the only parent—are employed.
- Help families deal with issues raised by social trends, such as mobility, sexual permissiveness, and individualism.

- Help couples who are in pain and considering divorce.
- Help divorced couples avoid behavior that is destructive to parent-child and other family relationships.
- Help families who are entering or leaving a community.
- Be sensitive to the economic pressures families experience.
- Be sensitive to the family situations of church employees.
- Be aware of the influences that shape personal and family values and behaviors.
- Address policies, programs, ministries, and services to families of different cultural, ethnic, and religious heritages, and build programs on the strengths of these traditions.

(Adapted from USSC,
A Family Perspective in Church and Society, p. 10)

APPENDIX E

Developmental Needs
of Adolescents and Young Adults

Youth ministry must take into account young people's unique developmental needs as they grow toward maturity. Ask yourself if youth ministry programs and activities are designed in a way that takes into account the individual developmental needs within stages of growth. Also ask whether those who are ministering to the pastoral needs of young people, whether they be youth ministers, pastors, teachers, catechists, scout leaders, coaches, and so on, are attuned to the developmental needs specific to each age-group. Research has identified the following dimensions of human life in which the developmental needs of young people take place:

- physical activity
- competence and achievement
- identity
- creativity and career
- relationships
- structure and autonomy
- meaningful participation
- spirituality
- sexuality

(The above categories are adapted from those presented in *3:00 to 6:00 P.M.: Young Adolescents at Home and in the Community,* by Leah M. Lefstein et al., pp. 13–17, and *Sharing IV* [Winona, MN: Saint Mary's Press, 1988], by Thomas Zanzig, pp. 57–58.)

The following is a summary of the developmental needs of each age-group and the implication of those needs for youth ministry. Each section is organized around the dimensions given above.

Young Adolescents

Physical activity: Young adolescents are known, generally, for their boundless and extensive energy. But they are also unpredictable. At one time they seem never to be able to stop, while at other times they seem never to be able to get started. Young growing bodies need time to relax as well as time to exercise and stretch. If young people complain about exercise, it may be because growing muscles and bones can be painful even without movement and activity.

The diversity in development of young teenagers requires a sensitivity to and consideration of their strength, coordination, and size. Intense, competitive physical activities often place a lot of stress on those who mature later as opposed to "early bloomers." Physical activity in groups or teams is encouraged because it enables young people to work together and avoids exposing them to the potential embarrassment of one-to-one competition.

Competence and achievement: Succeeding at a task can be just the thing young adolescents need to help them gain self-confidence, especially if the achievement warrants and receives admiration. Programs need to include success-oriented activities. Improving skills and mastering new ones helps build confidence and allow for nonthreatening and appropriate risk taking. Make sure that commitments are short term and provide easy exits. Self-confidence helps allay some of the self-consciousness of early adolescents. The usual result is an increase in desirable behavior.

However, while young people need to prove to themselves—and to others—that they are capable and competent to do things well, they also need to discover that they can survive disappointment when things do not go as planned.

Self-definition: The task of determining who they are as individuals can be unsettling for young adolescents. Opportunities that help them define and understand themselves and how they fit into society are important. At this age they are no longer content to be only observers in their ever-widening world; they also want to be participants.

Creative expression: Young adolescents will express what they are feeling whether we like it or not. Their music, hairstyles, clothes, and behavior are most often expressions of their hopes, dreams, fears, and worries. In the way they express themselves, they are a diverse group; some are outgoing, others are shy. Some of them express themselves well verbally, and others do not. In whatever way they may do it, expressing what is going on inside of them enables them to understand who they are becoming.

Offering creative ways to express their feelings, such as poetry, art, creative writing, and acting, can help channel their energy in a positive fashion. In addition to the arts, other ways they might express themselves creatively are synchronized swimming, Rollerblading, tending a garden, making bread, and the like.

Positive interaction with adults and peers: Studies show that parents still are the primary source young people turn to for advice, affection, and values. But, at this independence-seeking age, other significant adults take on important roles as sources of advice and conversation apart from parents. Adults who work with young adolescents need to be willing to share feelings and values with them. They need to know how to strike up a conversation, to make the young person feel at ease, and to model what they believe. Taking advantage of opportunities for positive interaction with adults can be seen as markers of growing maturity in early adolescents as they move toward adulthood.

Development of positive relationships with peers also ranks high on the agendas of young teenagers. It is with complete amazement (and oftentimes dismay) that adults watch these young people talk for endless hours on the phone to peers that they have seen and talked to all day in school. Opportunities for developing warm and trusting relationships between young people and their peers, such as slumber parties and lock-ins, are important youth ministry activities for this age-group.

Structure and clear limits: In his book *Director's Manual for the Discovering Program,* Michael Carotta describes the need of young adolescents for structure in this way:

> Imagine swimming in an ocean with no sight of land. Or imagine driving on a highway with no dividing lines, traffic lights, one-way indicators, or speed regulations. . . . The complete novice might either refuse to engage in the activities or, worse, attempt them but panic when it becomes clear that she or he is unprepared for the task at hand. So it is for the young adolescent who is learning how to move from childhood toward adulthood but is given no guidance for the journey. Young people need and want structure and clear limits for their behavior, and it is the responsibility of caring adults to provide them with such guidance.

> Because adolescents so often seem overtly and emotionally opposed to structure and clear limits, adults might feel reluctant to provide them. . . . The fact is that young people, despite their protests to the contrary, appreciate the help of structure and clear limits.

> Structure and clear limits benefit young adolescents in at least three ways.
> - They relieve young people of the task of constantly making decisions about their behavior, decisions that not only are difficult to make but also carry the risk of embarrassment or failure. . . .
> - They help young people . . . persevere in their various efforts, which in turn helps them succeed, and such success then leads to an increase in self-esteem.

> - They help young people feel safe in their activities, and such security can empower them to live with joy and confidence.

> Of course, some young people will choose to test . . . the structure or . . . the limits provided by adults. When doing so, however, they will know exactly where they stand. Some young people will choose to swim into dangerously deep waters, but if we provide clear guidance, they will . . . know where to find land when they need it. Some will certainly drive on the wrong side of the road, but as long as we keep the dividing line and the traffic signals clearly visible, they will know where the safe side of the street is when they want to return to it. Failure to provide structure and clear limits only leaves young people anxious and confused. (Pp. 22–23)

Meaningful participation: Young adolescents need to have increasingly significant roles in deciding and planning what goes on in their lives. For youth ministry this means young people should participate in deciding and planning their programs and take on leadership roles in carrying them out. They want and need a way to practice what they are learning and need to use their developing skills.

Adults involved with this group need to be careful that the responsibilities delegated and the involvement expected is in keeping with the maturity level of the young people or the group. Delegation of leadership and responsibility must be gradual. Care should be taken to not expect too much, too fast; to not set up the young people for failure. Remember that the attention span of this group is relatively short, and therefore, time commitments to the tasks delegated should also be short.

Personal spiritual experience: Beginning to think abstractly opens a whole new world for young people, especially with regard to their personal spiritual experience. Faith questions begin to haunt them: Is there really a God? What is God like? Maybe all this stuff about God really is not true. What happens after I or someone who is important to me dies? Beliefs held to be true in the past, especially those of parents, are often challenged and tested.

Young people need permission, even encouragement, to question their beliefs. With understanding and guidance these doubts and questions can be the beginnings of a personal faith that is their own. Teenagers need adults who will walk beside them and model, rather than preach, religious convictions. They need faith-filled adults who accept their challenges, allow for questioning, and who genuinely care for them.

Discovering sexuality: The onset of puberty affects the whole being of young adolescents. Most directly, though, there is an awakening of the sexual aspect of their personhood, which they need to make sense of. From within them comes an explosion of feelings coupled with questions: Why do I feel so happy or so sad? Why am I so attracted to this person and always want to be near him or her? Is it normal to feel as sexually excited as I am? Why is everyone else developing physically while I'm not? Am I gay because of how I feel? Do I try to direct my sexual feelings according to what I believe is right, or do I go along with what the media seem to be saying?

Understanding their sexuality is important because the unknown produces fear in early adolescents. This fear can impede most of the areas of their development, and can produce inappropriate behavior. Early adolescents not only need opportunities to gain an understanding of their sexual development and the physical and emotional changes connected to them, but they also need appropriate ways to express their sexual energy. Again, they need open and honest acceptance from healthy, caring adults to help them understand their emerging sexuality and to express it in appropriate ways.

(With the exception of the sections on structure, spirituality, and sexuality, the preceding material on young adolescents is adapted from *3:00 to 6:00 P.M.: Planning Programs for Young Adolescents,* by Gayle Dorman, pp. 43–45.)

Older Adolescents

Physical activity: Rapid growth and development has somewhat stabilized for older adolescents, and the changes in their bodies have been accepted for the most part. They are beginning to realize that they are capable of great strength, stamina, and perseverance. For many, they are now stronger and larger than their parents. They have gained an understanding of how their physical being functions and how it can affect all the areas of their life.

Older adolescents continue to need physical activity, to gain confidence in their physical capabilities, and to learn new skills. Collaboration and teamwork in physical activities can help them feel good about their physical self, and provide fulfillment and enjoyment. Healthy physical activity and involvement can help channel some of their strong emotional and sexual feelings.

Competence and achievement: Most older adolescents have overcome self-consciousness about their new self, although they can still have strong feelings of an "imaginary audience" looking at them. They are now able to make commitments that are more long term.

The achievements of the younger years are being replaced with new ones: getting a license and driving a car, obtaining a job, earning money in order to do what they want. Older adolescents have a need to prove themselves that sometimes involves risk taking in their driving, substance abuse, or sexual activity.

This age-group needs to be challenged to take responsibility for failures as well as successes and to learn how to grow from such experiences.

Identity: Older adolescents, generally, have moved beyond puberty and its roller coaster ride of defining who they are. However, there is a continued need to recognize their own unique personhood. For older adolescents, identity formation becomes more internal than external; it now takes place most often in the context of personal, one-on-one relationships, or even in time alone for personal reflection.

Activities that nurture this new perspective, such as one-on-one discussions, quiet time, reflection, journal writing, and solitude, should be considered.

Creativity and career: Young adolescents' creative expression focuses on learning new skills. For older adolescents, it involves using these skills to discover new worlds, discern areas of new interests and talents, and envision a future. Acting, singing, dancing, reading, and writing poems, diaries, journals, or letters are now ways of gaining a better understanding of the gifts and talents they have been given. They can also be opportunities for searching for a career or vocation.

Positive relationships with peers and adults: Gaining positive relationships with our peers and those outside that group is a lifelong developmental task. For older adolescents, a good healthy relationship with an adult can be just the boost of confidence that they need at that moment. There is a real need to have someone older, who is trusted, that they can talk to and confide in if needed—someone who has survived the turbulence of adolescence, someone to give them hope. Adults need to realize that this type of relationship does not mean that they are "buddies" with the adolescent or that they must act like a teenager, but that the young person clearly knows that they care for them.

Sharing dreams, stories, and experiences with peers is paramount. Newly acquired driver's licenses mean spending countless hours together, going to ball games, the movies, or parties, or just driving around. Home is usually the last place older adolescents can be found. Youth ministry for older adolescents needs plenty of opportunities for safe, quality interaction with peers.

Structure and autonomy: As young people move into older adolescence they need more and more to test and to try new things, but not to operate completely in the unknown. Structure and clear limits take on the character of guidelines rather than hard and fast rules. Older adolescents need to set some rules for themselves, to develop a sense of autonomy and responsibility. They need to be able to make an increasing number of decisions for themselves, and to learn their limits from the consequences of their actions.

Meaningful participation: Older adolescents are capable of managing significant roles in the programs they participate in, especially if a program is one in which they have previously been a participant. A team or mentor relationship with an adult is an especially effective way to give them the support they need while allowing them to participate in a meaningful way.

Spirituality: Older adolescents are capable of profound experiences of God. They begin to shape a faith that is relational and interpersonal, sometimes at the expense of their relationship with the church and the traditional beliefs passed on by their family. God becomes a personal God who knows them intimately, accepts them, and loves them unconditionally. God is experienced in the people they love more than in what they learn about God.

Older adolescents are looking for ways to make a difference in the world, and oftentimes are not sure if the institutional church provides the context for such aspirations. They need opportunities that provide deep spiritual experiences in which they can nurture an intimate relationship with God and relationships with believing adults who maintain a connection with the church.

Understanding sexuality: For most older adolescents, the majority of the physical and emotional changes that happen throughout puberty have come to a stop. Now comes the task of making sense of their role as a sexual being. How do they relate to people in light of their sexuality? Does their gender affect vocational choices that are available? How does their maleness or femaleness affect their relationships?

They need to know that it is normal to have strong sexual desires or seemingly none at all; that sexuality cannot be measured by group norms; that they are okay, even if they are not dating at all while their friends date all the time.

Young Adults

Physical activity: For the young adult, physical activity is seen more in the context of a planned leisure activity, a way of staying in shape, an opportunity for recreating and socializing. Spas, athletic leagues, clubs, or dance lessons are places to meet new people and enjoy the activity. Physical activity continues to harness sexual feelings and emotions as a productive outlet, and can be a way of being intimate with others without engaging in sexual activity. A youth ministry program for young adults should include opportunities for physical activities, especially if these are not available elsewhere.

Becoming competent: Acquiring the knowledge and skills to get things done is important to young adults. It gives them the feeling that they are able to cope with whatever life throws at them and enables them to choose positive ways to carry out the tasks to which they are committed. Effective young adult ministry should affirm the competencies that young adults already have and provide opportunities for the young adults to transfer their sense of competency to other areas of their life.

Forming personal identity: Young adulthood is a time to come to grips with the person one has become, to be comfortable with oneself, and to allow people to see the real person inside. It is a time to get rid of masks, to be real, to recognize and strive for integrity between what one believes and how one acts. Young adults experience a lot of vulnerability in removing masks and allowing others to see their true self; and they need support and encouragement in this task.

Creativity and career: For young adults, creativity is expressed through initial job and career choices. Being creative is integrating what they are good at and what gives them personal satisfaction; is discerning what kind of career fits their values and contributes to their sense of personal integrity; is developing a holistic approach to life that incorporates all that they are. Young adults should also be able to creatively express themselves in the work they have chosen to do. If this does not happen, they need to redefine their career and look at other options.

Young adult ministry should provide a supportive atmosphere for reflection on self, for defining and redefining career, and for considering creative options, especially in regard to a possible career choice of ministry in the church.

Relationships: As young adults become more secure with their identity, they grow in their ability to relate with others and establish true friendships. Developing capacities that foster true friendship—openness, trust, forgiveness, and compassion—is one of their primary tasks. The development of these capacities opens the way for commitment to lifelong relationships of caring, interdependency, and true intimacy.

Structure and autonomy: At this age there is a shift from the independence of the adolescent to the interdependence of the young adult. The freedom and choice essential to interdependent relationships need to be encouraged. Likewise, the young adult's relationship with the church should also be interdependent, a relationship that is characterized by freedom and choice.

Any unhealthy dependency at this time feels stifling and smothering, whether one is depending on others, or others are depending on oneself. It is important for young adults to be able to recognize unhealthy dependence in relationships and to move toward interdependence.

Community: With the development of their personal and interpersonal skills, young adults need to be challenged to see that they are responsible to more than just themselves. The challenge is to be an active citizen and participant as a member of the civil and church communities. Sharing their gifts and talents needs to be seen as important for their continued growth.

Young adults are capable of, and will feel good about, participating in programs and activities that will meet their needs and those of their peers. Making a difference in the lives of younger people can be especially satisfying, giving the young adult a feeling of worth and connection that comes from passing on hope and faith to a new generation.

Spirituality: Separation from the family has a tremendous impact on young adults, whether they are going away to school or acquiring a residence of their own. They suddenly have the opportunity to choose their behavior and are personally challenged to maintain an integrity between their behavior and their beliefs.

Many young adults take some type of "moratorium" from the moral values instilled in them by their family and tend to express their new freedom by acting the opposite of them. This discord is usually temporary, and it is important to show patient care and concern for them during this time.

Young adults are often disconnected from their church and may actually resist any type of organized religion until they get married and have children of their own. At the same time, they are vulnerable to other faiths or unhealthy cults. Programs and activities should be offered by way of invitation, respecting their choice, yet giving a clear message of caring and welcome. There should be a maturity evident in any youth ministry aimed at young adults, which allows them to decide about and personally own their faith.

Sexuality: Integrating sexuality into their life is a key issue for young adults. The values that they espouse in regard to sexuality and sexual expression reflect their total value system. The ability to be intimate while maintaining moral and personal integrity is a great challenge in today's society, but young adults need to know that it is possible, and that it is a key to personal happiness. Likewise, young adults will be faced with issues of sexual discrimination, perhaps even harassment, in the workplace, in higher education, and even in the church. Such issues include the inequity of salaries and employment opportunities, the possibilities for study, and the opportunities for ministerial roles. Young adults will need the sensitivity to recognize these issues, and the skills and encouragement to resolve them.

(The preceding material on young adults is adapted from *Sharing IV,* by Thomas Zanzig, pp. 57–58.)

APPENDIX F

Developing a Youth Ministry Mission Statement

1. At the top of a sheet of newsprint write in capital letters WE BELIEVE. The planners should then spend some time brainstorming (not analyzing or discussing) all their different beliefs about young people and what the parish wants for them.

2. Once the list is exhausted, another sheet of newsprint should be put up with the statement WE SERVE at the top. Brainstorm what and who it is that the parish serves through total youth ministry. For example: Do you serve senior high school students? junior high school students? young adults? Does the youth ministry effort include families? Is there outreach to young people in the broader community or only to those within the parish?

3. Finally, on another sheet of newsprint, brainstorm a third section, THEREFORE WE DO. List all the things the parish should do in order to serve the young people they believe in.

4. Once the group has finished brainstorming, some time should be spent on discussion. If any items are listed that the group as a whole cannot come to an agreement on, they should be dropped.

5. When a consensus has been reached, the lists of information should then be given to someone delegated to write a mission statement that effectively expresses what the group as a whole surfaced.

6. A reflection sheet, that is, a copy of the mission statement draft with questions pertaining to it, should be mailed out to the whole youth ministry commission. The letter to the commission members should instruct them to do the following:
- Read the mission statement.
- Respond to the questions on the reflection sheet.
- Bring the reflection sheet to the next commission meeting.

7. In setting the agenda for the next commission meeting, the discussion and approval of the mission statement should be placed under new business.

8. At the commission meeting, go around the table and ask members to share their responses from the reflection sheet. The youth ministry coordinator and the pastor should be present for this sharing.

9. After hearing the responses, the commission should consider three alternatives:

- Reaffirm the statement as it is.
- Reaffirm the statement with minor changes.
- Reject the statement and do a total rewrite.

10. If the commission calls for a revision or rewrite, have the person who drafted the initial statement complete the task. Make certain that the person has all the comments made at that meeting. Place the mission statement on the next month's meeting agenda under old business. Again, the commission should be prepared by way of a mailing to act on the revised statement.

APPENDIX G

Using a Consensus-Seeking Process

The purpose of a consensus-seeking process is to clarify the feelings and intentions of group members so that the level of agreement about a position, decision, or proposal regarding a particular issue can be determined. Each member of the group uses a scale to determine his or her degree of agreement or disagreement and then shares that result with the group, by either a secret or a public vote. The voting scale is as follows:

+3 Total agreement with the position, decision, or proposal. The person feels that this is the only way to go. No other choice is possible.

+2 Total agreement with the position, decision, or proposal. The person would accept another option only if the whole group called for it.

+1 Agreement with the position, decision, or proposal. The person is without strong conviction, and agrees simply because others agree with it.

0 Neutral. The person does not see any clear direction, or does not understand the issue, or does not have strong beliefs either way.

–1 Disagreement with the position, decision, or proposal. The person has questions about its validity or appropriateness.

–2 Total disagreement with the position, decision, or proposal. The person believes strongly that it is not good for herself or himself or for the whole group, but will accept it if the group calls for it.

–3 Total disagreement with the position, decision, or proposal. A person choosing this value feels strongly that this cannot happen as proposed. This level says that the position, decision, or proposal is not possible and cannot be supported in any way.

Calculate whether the group as a whole stands in favor of, or in opposition to, the position, decision, or proposal. Do this by adding the numbers of the plus votes, subtracting the numbers of the minus votes and dividing the result by the number of people in the group. If the result is a plus number, the group as a whole stands in favor of the position, decision, or proposal. If the result is a minus number, the group as a whole stands in opposition to it. The size of the number will indicate the degree to which the group is for or against the position, decision, or proposal.

Any casting of a level 3 vote, either + or –, that is contrary to the average stand of the group indicates that more work is required before a consensus can be claimed.

Any casting of a level 2 vote, either + or –, that is contrary to the average stand of the group means that more discussion may be needed. But, for example, even with a level 2 dissent, a pretty clear consensus can be claimed if the group's overall stand is 1.5 or more in favor.

Before using this process, those participating should be encouraged to exaggerate their tendencies at first, going toward the extremes. For example, a vote of –3 can be changed to –2 in a second balloting, but if no –3 appears, there may not be a second try.

APPENDIX H

Three Models for Selecting Youth Ministry Commission Members

The Discernment Model

The discernment model is one way to select youth ministry commission members in the parish. It seeks the broadest possible input from the community and incorporates prayer, reflection, and discussion during each step of the process.

The discernment process has a number of benefits. The most evident benefit is that participants usually find the process affirming, supportive, and unifying. There are no losers and winners. The whole parish is involved in the process. Those chosen have a strong mandate and are supported by a large majority. A sense of the broad distribution of gifts and talents in the community is surfaced.

A step-by-step description of the discernment model follows. In this description the pastoral council is responsible for facilitating most of the process. The youth ministry commission members are nominated as part of an overall process for nominating people for membership in all parish leadership or governing bodies.

1. Designate a Sunday as Nomination Sunday. Before that Sunday, by way of the parish bulletin or a mailing, inform the parishioners of the membership positions that will be vacant in parish leadership and governing bodies, along with a description of the function of the bodies and the skills and talents needed in the people who will fill the positions.

2. In conjunction with Nomination Sunday's liturgies, invite all those assembled to pray, reflect, and then submit the names of persons that they believe can represent them for the various parish leadership and governing bodies, including the youth ministry commission. Then contact the people who are nominated to see if they are willing to serve. Nominees who accept are not yet committed to being a member of the commission but rather commit themselves to attending an orientation session and to continuing the discernment process.

3. Ask members who are willing to attend the orientation and discernment session to prepare a brief statement describing their experience with and concern for the young people of the parish. Along with that they should submit some brief biographical information. In the meantime the parish is

asked to continue to pray for those who have accepted nomination.

4. Conduct the orientation and discernment session in a room that is pleasant, warm, and conducive to prayerful sharing. Begin with shared prayer. The designated leader then talks about the purposes and functions of a youth ministry commission, describing the different tasks that need to be performed. Job descriptions are given to each of those involved.

5. Invite each candidate to share a bit of her or his own faith and what gifts she or he might bring to the youth ministry commission. After each is allowed to share, there should be another opportunity for prayer or a blessing of the candidates.

6. Ask nominees to declare if they are willing to serve on the commission. If there are more people willing to serve than the number of positions available, a selection process needs to be used.

7. The selection process consists of the nominees completing a ballot with the names of the persons who they feel would be most effective as commission members. The persons whose names are written the most times are the ones selected and their names are announced to the group. All the candidates are thanked for offering their services to the church, and those not discerned as members are encouraged to be involved with the work of the youth ministry commission.

8. Members of the commission (as well as all other parish structures) should be installed at an appropriate liturgy celebrated by the assembled parish community.

The Election Model

The election model is another way to select people to serve on the youth commission.

1. A nomination procedure should be carried out by informing the parish of the positions that need to be filled and providing an opportunity to submit nominations.

2. As in the discernment process, the membership committee (or its equivalent) should contact the persons nominated to find out if they are willing to

serve. If so, they are asked to put together a biographical sketch and a statement of what they hope to see accomplished as a member.

3. The nomination committee prepares a slate of candidates that includes each candidate's biographical sketch and statement of purpose. These are typed and attached to the parish ballot.

4. At each of the liturgies of a designated weekend, the parishioners are given an opportunity to vote for the persons that they feel would be most qualified. The membership committee tallies the votes and informs the parish of the results at an appropriate time.

5. As in the discernment process, the youth ministry commission members who are elected should be installed at a regular Sunday liturgy along with members of other parish bodies.

The Appointment Model

Finally, the appointment model would be the most appropriate way to select youth ministry commission members when the commission is initially formed. But for the sake of involving the whole parish in youth ministry affairs, the other two models are recommended for subsequent selection of commission members.

1. Candidates are nominated by an official group within the parish, such as the pastoral council, the youth ministry staff, or any group that might have a good sense of the skills and qualities needed to serve effectively on the youth ministry commission.

2. Once a list of candidates is established, their willingness to serve on the commission needs to be verified.

3. From among the candidates willing to serve, the pastoral council or the pastor appoints members to the commission.

4. As in the other two models, the members should be installed in the presence of the parish community at an appropriate liturgy.

APPENDIX I

An Annual Calendar of Tasks
for a Youth Ministry Commission

The following list of agenda items represents the common tasks and duties that a youth ministry commission is responsible for. They are arranged according to the time of year they occur. This calendar is based on a July-to-June administrative year. Usual procedure has the officers discussing the agenda before the commission meeting and making sure that all the information necessary for action is available at the meeting.

July

1. Appoint a committee to prepare the annual report. Each year the commission prepares an annual report to present to the pastoral council and the parish staff. It appoints a committee to draft the report. The report includes an end-of-year financial statement, an overview of all programs, activities, and events, and a narrative summary of the objectives achieved and of significant issues that surfaced. It should be presented to the commission in August.

2. Select the leadership. Before the July meeting, the nomination and election committee prepares a process for selecting commission officers for the following year. The selection process is part of the July meeting.

3. Charge the education and formation committee. The committee responsible for the education and formation of the commission is charged to draft and submit a plan for ongoing education and formation of the commission throughout the year. The plan should be presented to the commission in August.

4. Charge the nomination and election committee. The nomination and election committee is directed to plan a ceremony for installing new officers at the August commission meeting. The installation should be done in the context of prayer as well as fun. Special refreshments might be included.

August

1. Install the commission leadership. The commission members participate in the commissioning ceremony as assigned. The installation ceremony could be a part of the opening prayer, thus allowing the new chairperson to conduct the official business of the meeting.

2. Review and accept the youth ministry commission calendar. Before the August meeting, the executive committee should prepare a calendar of all commission meetings, special meetings, retreats, days of reflection, or in-service meetings that the members of the youth ministry commission will be expected to attend. The calendar is presented to the commission at the August meeting for review and approval.

3. Present the youth ministry action plans. The youth ministry coordinator presents an outline of all the programs, activities, and events to be offered for young people during the year. The report should include a brief explanation of the existing programs, new programs, and programs that are being discontinued. If the youth ministry plans have resulted as part of a long-range planning process, they will have already been approved and no formal action will be needed. The commission, however, might want to show their support again by giving their approval.

4. Appoint members to standing committees. The chairperson of the commission should decide and obtain consent from the members before the August meeting for their active participation on standing committees— committees such as executive, nomination and election, budget, policy review, long-range planning, assessment, and education and formation. At appropriate times, a charge should be written for each committee. The commission as a whole affirms committee appointments and votes on committee charges. The chairperson formally appoints the members of the committees and formally charges them with their duties.

5. Review and approve the annual report. The committee that has prepared the annual report presents it to the commission for review and approval. Once approved, the report is presented to the pastoral council at its regular meeting.

6. Approve the plan for education and formation. The education and formation committee presents for approval its plan for the education and formation of the commission.

September

Charge the assessment committee. The assessment committee is charged to assess the effectiveness of the youth ministry coordinator's accomplishment of the job description. During the next month the committee determines a process for assessment and schedules meetings with the coordinator to carry out this assessment. The assessment should be completed by January.

October

1. Review the budget. The chairperson of the finance committee reviews with the whole commission the quarterly financial report (July to September). This review gives the commission an idea of how expenditures relate to the approved budget, as well as how the youth ministry program stands fiscally.

2. Charge the policy review committee. The policy review committee is charged to review youth ministry policies. After consulting with the youth ministry coordinator, the committee prepares recommendations on policies that might need to be added, revised, or revoked. This should be done by the November meeting.

November

Listen to the policy review committee's report. The policy review committee reports to the commission on its findings regarding the youth ministry policies.

December

1. Evaluate commission meetings. Before the December commission meeting, the executive committee decides on a method to evaluate the commission meetings. If evaluation instruments are used, they should be distributed to the commission members at this meeting. Members might take time at the December meeting to fill out the evaluation and return it immediately, or they may do so at the next meeting. Midyear is a good time to make any adaptations that the evaluations might suggest.

2. Request a letter of intent from the youth ministry coordinator. The youth ministry coordinator is requested to submit a letter before the January meeting, stating intent for recontracting or for nonrenewal.

January

1. Approve of recommendations from the assessment committee. The assessment committee makes an evaluative report to the commission regarding the youth minister's accomplishment of the job description. The committee also makes recommendations for job description changes as well as for renewal or nonrenewal of the youth minister's contract. Because this is a personnel matter, it should be conducted in closed session with only commission members present.

2. Report on the youth ministry coordinator's letter of intent. If a letter of intent to recontract or to not renew the contract was requested from the current coordinator of youth ministry following the December committtee meeting, a report of the coordinator's response is given.

3. Review the current year's objectives. With the first half of the fiscal year completed, the commission should discuss the progress of the current objectives in light of the mission statement and three-year goals.

The youth ministry coordinator provides information and data on accomplishments of the objectives up to this point. If objectives have not been written for all three years of the long-range plan, the commission appoints a planning committee to write the objectives for the coming year. The coordinator helps with this.

4. Review the budget and financial statement. The chairperson of the finance committee presents a mid-year review of the youth ministry budget, including projected and actual expenses and projected and actual income. This review is for the information of the commission, and no further action is necessary.

5. Review the evaluation of the commission meetings. The commission discusses the findings of the evaluation of commission meetings by the members and determines if any changes need to be made at meetings.

February

1. Review and approve next year's objectives. The commission discusses the objectives that were written for next year and approves them. Then the coordinator is charged with the task of getting action plans written. The coordinator, along with the members of the youth ministry staff, writes the action plans. (This process is described further in chapter 5.) This task should be completed by April.

2. Charge the finance committee. The finance committee is charged to develop a budget for the coming fiscal year in accordance with the long-range plan. The coordinator and the youth ministry team should be involved in the budget development.

3. Decide whether to renew or not renew the youth ministry coordinator's contract. If the commission votes to renew the youth ministry coordinator's contract, a contract negotiating committee is appointed to negotiate the terms for renewal. If the contract is not to be renewed, the process for contracting a new coordinator should be initiated (see chapter 6).

March

1. Charge the nomination and election committee. The nomination and election committee is charged to coordinate and conduct the commission membership elections in May. The commission nominations and elections should be done in coordination with nominations and elections to other parish organizations, such as the board of education or the pastoral council. The committee should have a slate of candidates ready for the May elections.

2. Charge the education and formation committee to provide for the training of new commission members.

3. Discuss and approve next year's budget. The finance committee presents to the commission its recommended budget for the next year. The commission discusses the budget, asks questions, makes any needed amendments, approves it, and then instructs a commission member to present it to the pastoral council and parish finance council at the next council meeting. The council will approve or reject the budget's bottom line.

4. Approve the contract for the youth ministry coordinator. If the coordinator's contract is to be renewed, the contract negotiating committee presents to the commission a contract proposal for approval. It should include salary, benefits, job description, and so forth. Once the contract proposal is approved, a formal contract is drawn up for signing. Arrangements should be made for the contract to be signed by the youth ministry coordinator, the commission chairperson, the pastoral council chairperson, and the pastor. This activity is usually done outside of the commission meeting and, once it is finalized, a report is given to the commission in April. If the coordinator's contract is not being renewed, the process for hiring a new coordinator continues.

April

1. Hear the report on the contract signing of the youth ministry coordinator. The chairperson informs the commission whether the contract has been accepted and signed by the coordinator.

2. Review next year's action plans. The commission reviews the action plans put together by the coordinator and the youth ministry team and makes any recommendations for change.

May

1. Hear the report on the pastoral council's review of the youth ministry budget. If the council has rejected the budget, the commission should ask why, as well as what guidelines need to be met.

2. Choose a youth ministry commission slate for parish elections. If the parish elects members for the various governing structures during May, the commission nominees can be included with other parish organization slates. If no general parish election process is set up, the commission determines and carries out the process for electing its members.

3. Charge the education and formation committee. A charge is given to the education and formation committee to acquaint the new commission members with the responsibilities of the commission. A packet of information that gives an overview of all the workings of the commission can be assembled and distributed. Have the committee invite the newly elected members of the commission to observe the June meeting.

June

1. Train new commission members. The members of the commission should introduce themselves. The experienced members should also describe any responsibilities they have assumed in leadership or on the various youth ministry committees. Reserve time at the end of the meeting to solicit and respond to any questions the newly elected members might have.

2. Review the goals and objectives of the current year. The commission reviews the accomplishments of the objectives for the year and the degree to which goals have been reached. Strengths and weaknesses are identified for possible inclusion in the annual report, which will go to the pastoral council.

3. Plan for the parish installation of new commission members. The new commission members should be installed along with the new members of other parish leadership structures. If no general installation is planned for members of parish organizations, the commission arranges for the installation of its new members, preferably at a Sunday liturgy.

APPENDIX J

Interview Guidelines

Definition of an Interview

An interview is a conversation between a candidate and an employer to discuss the possibility of the candidate's filling the employer's job opening.

Purpose of an Interview

For the Employer
- to determine if the applicant has sufficient qualifications to fill the job opening
- to clarify or supplement information on the candidate's resume
- to give the applicant essential information about the job opening and about the parish

For the Applicant
- to determine if the applicant's competencies correspond to the needs of the parish
- to determine if this is the type of place where the applicant could work effectively
- to determine if the resources provided by the employer are adequate for the applicant to meet the requirements of the job

Points to Remember

- Review background data on the candidate before the interview.
- Check references before the interview.
- Know what you are looking for in an applicant: qualifications, qualities, and so forth.
- Have your interview questions prepared ahead of time.
- Do not waste time on factual questions whose answers are in the resume.
- Ask open-ended questions beginning with *why, when, who, what,* or *where.*
- Do not imply that a response was poor or inadequate.
- Do not put the candidate on the defensive; do not argue with or confuse the applicant.
- Respect the individuality of the applicant and try to preserve his or her self-confidence.
- Do not ask leading questions or give away the answer you want.
- Do not let the applicant oversell you. Often persons are hired because of their verbal fluency and ability to sell themselves. The best talker may not be the best worker.
- Listen and then talk.
- Come to an agreement with the applicant on a timeline for making a decision.
- Write down reactions as soon as possible after the interview.
- Remember that applicants are also interviewing you to see if this is a place where they would want to work.

For Further Reading

Part A: Foundations for Parish Youth Ministry

Bowman, Thea, ed. *Families: Black and Catholic, Catholic and Black*. Washington, DC: United States Catholic Conference (USCC), 1985.

Campolo, Anthony. *Growing Up in America: A Sociology of Youth Ministry*. Grand Rapids, MI: Zondervan, 1989.

Dorman, Gayle. *3:00 to 6:00 P.M.: Planning Programs for Young Adolescents*. Carrboro, NC: Center for Early Adolescence, 1985.

Ekstrom, Reynolds R. *Access Guide to Pop Culture*. New Rochelle, NY: Don Bosco Multimedia, 1989.

Elizondo, Virgilio P. *Galilean Journey: The Mexican American Promise*. Maryknoll, NY: Orbis Books, 1983.

Elkind, David. *All Grown Up and No Place to Go*. Reading, MA: Addison-Wesley, 1984.

———. *The Hurried Child*. Reading, MA: Addison-Wesley, 1981.

Farel, Anita M. *Early Adolescence and Religion*. Carrboro, NC: Center for Early Adolescence, 1982.

Forliti, John. *Growing Together: An Opportunity for Young Adolescents and Their Parents*. Washington, DC: NCEA, 1984.

Gleason, Kenneth, Kevin Jones-Prendergast, Marilyn Kielbasa, and David M. Riley. *Ministries Growing Together: Resources for Integrating Adolescent Religious Education with Youth Ministry*. Winona, MN: Saint Mary's Press, 1992.

Greinacher, Norbert, and Virgil Elizondo, eds. *The Transmission of the Faith to the Next Generation*. Edinburgh, Scotland: T. and T. Clark, 1984.

John Paul II. *"Christi Fidelis Laici."* Washington, DC: USCC, 1989.

———. *"To the Youth of the World."* Boston: Saint Paul's Editions, Daughters of Saint Paul, 1985.

Kimball, Don. *Power and Presence: A Theology of Relationships*. San Francisco: Harper and Row, 1987.

Lefstein, Leah M., and Joan Lipsitz. *3:00 to 6:00 P.M.: Programs for Young Adolescents*. Carrboro, NC: Center for Early Adolescence, 1983.

Lefstein, Leah M., et al. *3:00 to 6:00 P.M.: Young Adolescents at Home and in the Community*. Carrboro, NC: Center for Early Adolescence, 1982.

NFCYM. *The Challenge of Adolescent Catechesis: Maturing in Faith*. Washington, DC: NFCYM, 1986.

Ng, David. *Youth in the Community of Disciples*. Valley Forge, PA: Judson Press, 1984.

Ng, David, ed. *Asian Pacific American Youth Ministry*. Valley Forge, PA: Judson Press, 1988.

Paul VI. *Evangelii Nuntiandi*. Washington, DC: USCC, 1976.

Roberto, John, comp. *Readings in Youth Ministry*. Vol. 1, *Foundations*. Washington, DC: NFCYM, 1986.

Roberto, John, ed. *Faith Maturing: A Personal and Communal Task*. Washington, DC: NFCYM, 1985.

Shelton, Charles M. *Adolescent Spirituality*. Chicago: Loyola University Press, 1983.

Steinberg, Laurence D. *Understanding Families with Young Adolescents*. Carrboro, NC: Center for Early Adolescence, 1980.

Strommen, Merton P. *Five Cries of Youth*. Rev. ed. San Francisco: Harper and Row, 1988.

Strommen, Merton P., and A. Irene Strommen. *Five Cries of Parents*. San Francisco: Harper and Row, 1985.

Synod of Bishops. "The Synod Propositions." *Origins* 17 (31 December 1987): 499–509.

USCC. *A Family Perspective in Church and Society*. Washington, DC: USCC, 1988.

———. *Sharing the Light of Faith*. Washington, DC: USCC, 1979.

———. *A Vision of Youth Ministry*. Washington, DC: USCC, 1976, 1986.

Warren, Michael. *Faith, Culture, and the Worshiping Community*. New York: Paulist Press, 1989.

———. *Youth and the Future of the Church*. Minneapolis: Winston-Seabury, 1982.

Warren, Michael, ed. *Readings and Resources in Youth Ministry*. Winona, MN: Saint Mary's Press, 1987.

Part B: The Setup
for Parish Youth Ministry

Ambrose, Dub, and Walt Mueller. *Ministry to Families with Teenagers.* Loveland, CO: Group Publishing, 1988.

Beranek, Rudy. *Building a Rainbow.* Revised by Thomas J. Everson. Washington, DC: NFCYM, 1990.

Fox, Zeni, Marisa Guerin, Brian Reynolds, and John Roberto. *Leadership for Youth Ministry.* Winona, MN: Saint Mary's Press, 1984.

Harris, Maria. *Portrait of Youth Ministry.* New York: Paulist Press, 1981.

Holderness, Ginny W. *Youth Ministry—The Team Approach.* Atlanta: John Knox Press, 1980.

McCarty, Robert J., and Lynn Tooma. *Training Adults for Youth Ministry.* Winona, MN: Saint Mary's Press, 1990.

Rice, Wayne. *Junior High Ministry.* Grand Rapids, MI: Zondervan, 1987.

Roberto, John. *Adolescent Catechesis Resource Manual.* New York: Sadlier, 1988.

Roberto, John, and Reynolds R. Ekstrom. *Access Guide to Youth Evangelization.* New Rochelle, NY: Don Bosco Multimedia, 1989.

USCC. *A Pastoral Plan for Young Adult Ministry.* Washington, DC: USCC, 1980.

Warren, Michael. *Freeing Youth from the Systems: A New Agenda for Youth Ministry.* Kansas City, MO: Credence Cassettes/National Catholic Reporter Publishing, AA1425.

Part C: The Planning
and Maintaining
of Parish Youth Ministry

Bannon, William J., and Suzanne Donovan. *Volunteers and Ministry.* New York: Paulist Press, 1984.

Bimler, Richard W. *The Youth Group Meeting Guide.* Loveland, CO: Group Publishing, 1985.

Brown, Carolyn C. *Youth Ministries: Thinking Big with Small Groups.* Kansas City, MO: Abingdon Press, 1984.

Byer, James. *Becoming a Skilled Helper.* Six cassettes. Kansas City, MO: Credence Cassettes/National Catholic Reporter Publishing, AA1431.

Campolo, Anthony. *Ideas for Social Action.* El Cajon, CA: Youth Specialties, 1983.

Clark, Jean Illsely. *Who, Me Lead a Group?* Minneapolis: Winston Press, 1984.

Clinebell, Howard. *Basic Types of Pastoral Care and Counseling.* Nashville, TN: Abingdon Press, 1984.

Dues, Greg. *Called Together—Teen Motivation for Liturgy.* Dallas: Argus Communications, 1984.

Flagel, Clarice. *Avoiding Burnout.* Dubuque, IA: W. C. Brown, 1981.

Fox, Zeni, Marisa Guerin, Brian Reynolds, and John Roberto. *Leadership for Youth Ministry.* Winona, MN: Saint Mary's Press, 1984.

Griggs, Donald. *Planning for Teaching Church School.* Nashville, TN: Abingdon Press, 1985.

Hart, Thomas N. *The Art of Christian Listening.* New York: Paulist Press, 1980.

Keating, Charles J. *The Leadership Book.* New York: Paulist Press, 1982.

Kennedy, Eugene. *Crisis Counseling.* New York: Continuum, 1981.

Ng, David. *Developing Leaders for Youth Ministry.* Valley Forge, PA: Judson Press, 1984.

Rice, Wayne. *Great Ideas for Small Youth Groups.* El Cajon, CA: Youth Specialties, 1985.

Rice, Wayne, John Roberto, Mike Yaconelli, eds. Creative Resources for Youth Ministry. 3 vols. Winona, MN: Saint Mary's Press, 1991.

Rockers, Dolore, and Kenneth J. Pierre. *Shared Ministry.* Winona, MN: Saint Mary's Press, 1984.

Roehlkepartain, Eugene, ed. *The Youth Ministry Resource Book.* Loveland, CO: Group Publishing, 1988.

Sanford, John A. *Ministry Burnout.* New York: Paulist Press, 1982.

Sparks, Lee, ed. *The Youth Group How-to Book.* Loveland, CO: Group Publishing, 1984.

United Church of Christ, Office of Church Life and Leadership. *The Ministry of Volunteers.* Saint Louis: Office of Church Life and Leadership, United Church of Christ, 1979.

Van Ornum, William, and John B. Mordock. *Crisis Counseling with Children and Adolescents.* New York: Continuum, 1983.

Walters, Thomas P., ed. *Handbook for Parish Evaluation.* New York: Paulist Press, 1984.

Wilson, Marlene. *How to Mobilize Church Volunteers.* Minneapolis: Augsburg, 1983.

Index

Acknowledgments

The psalm verse on page 8 is from *Psalms Anew: In Inclusive Language,* compiled by Nancy Schreck and Maureen Leach (Winona, MN: Saint Mary's Press, 1986). Copyright © 1986 by Saint Mary's Press. All rights reserved.

Unless otherwise noted, the quotations on page 15 are from *A Vision of Youth Ministry,* 10th anniversary ed. (Washington, DC: United States Catholic Conference [USCC], 1986), pages 1, 7, 8, 9, and 10. Copyright © 1986 by USCC, Washington, D.C. Used with permission. All rights reserved. For a complete copy, call 1-800-235-8722.

The quotations on page 16 and the adapted material in appendices A and B are from *The Challenge of Adolescent Catechesis: Maturing in Faith* (Washington, DC: National Federation for Catholic Youth Ministry [NFCYM], 1986), pages 5, 8, 9–10, and 12–15. Copyright © 1986 by NFCYM, 3900-A Harewood Road NE, Washington, DC 20017. Used with permission. All rights reserved.

The diagram on page 18 is from *Power and Presence,* by Don Kimball (New York: Harper and Row, 1987), page 145. Copyright © 1987 by Don Kimball. Used with permission of the author.

The quotations on pages 19 and 20 are from *Readings in Youth Ministry,* vol. 1, *Foundations* (Washington, DC: NFCYM, 1986), pages 89–90, 97, and 101. Copyright © 1986 by NFCYM, 3700-A Oakview Terrace NE, Washington, DC 20017-2591. Used with permission. All rights reserved.

Appendix D is adapted from *A Family Perspective in Church and Society: A Manual for All Pastoral Leaders* (Washington, DC: USCC, 1987), page 10. Copyright © 1988 by USCC. Used with permission.

The material on young adolescents in appendix E, with the exception of sections as noted on page 103, is adapted from *3:00 to 6:00 P.M.: Planning Programs for Young Adolescents,* by Gayle Dorman (Carrboro, NC: Center for Early Adolescence, 1985), pages 43–45.

The excerpt on page 102 is from the *Director's Manual for the Discovering Program,* by Michael Carotta (Winona, MN: Saint Mary's Press, 1989), pages 22–23. Copyright © 1989 by Saint Mary's Press. All rights reserved.